THE
WAXMAN
REPORT

THE
WAXMAN
REPORT

How Congress Really Works

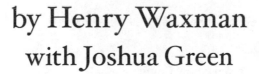

by Henry Waxman
with Joshua Green

TWELVE

NEW YORK   BOSTON

Twelve
Hachette Book Group
237 Park Avenue
New York, NY 10017

Visit our Web site at www.HachetteBookGroup.com.

Twelve is an imprint of Grand Central Publishing.
The Twelve name and logo are trademarks of Hachette Book Group, Inc.

Printed in the United States of America

First Edition: July 2009
10 9 8 7 6 5 4 3 2 1

Library of Congress Cataloging-in-Publication Data

Waxman, Henry
   The Waxman report: how Congress really works / Henry Waxman. —
   1st ed.
      p. cm.
   Includes index.
   ISBN 978-0-446-51925-0
   1. United States. Congress. House. 2. Waxman, Henry A. 3. Legislators—
   United States—Biography. 4. Legislators—California—Biography.
   5. United States—Politics and government—1945–1989. 6. United
   States—Politics and government—1989- I. Title.
   JK1319.W39 2009
   328.73092—dc22
                                                            2009006976

Book design by Charles Sutherland

To my wife and life-partner, Janet, whose love and devotion has been the single best thing that has happened to me; to my daughter, Shai Abramson; to my son, Michael Waxman, and daughter-in-law, Marjorie Waxman; and to my grandchildren, Ari, Maya and No'a Abramson, and Eva and Jacob Waxman, who mean the world to me.

CONTENTS

INTRODUCTION

During my thirty-five years in Congress, I've been involved in hundreds of hearings. Many were forgettable. A handful have had lasting impact. And one, on April 14, 1994, stands among the great Washington dramas. Like the McCarthy and Watergate hearings, it has assumed a place in popular mythology as a turning point in our national history that lives on in textbooks and Hollywood movies.

On that morning, in a hearing room of the House Energy and Commerce Committee, the CEOs of the nation's seven largest tobacco companies assembled for the first time to testify before Congress. I had summoned them there in my capacity as chairman of the Subcommittee on Health and the Environment to answer questions about the $61 billion industry they controlled and the 440,000 people who died every year as a result of its products. It was a showdown that had been years in the making.

The life of a congressman is often one of painstaking process. You endure the daily grind of committee meetings, markups, and hearings in order to build the foundation that all great legislation requires—from landmark measures like the New Deal, the Civil Rights Act, Medicare and Medicaid, to major new initiatives like climate change legislation and universal health care that could soon be enacted. You persevere so that those who abuse the public trust will be held to account. But mostly you do it for the rare and fleeting occasions when your actions might improve the lives of millions of your fellow Americans.

For years, tobacco had been a crisis that screamed out for government oversight, and as chairman of the House subcommittee responsible for overseeing the public health it was my job to address it. This didn't make me popular. A staffer for a Republican colleague from Virginia's tobacco country had an ashtray in his office with my picture at the bottom for stubbing out his cigarettes. But the Centers for Disease Control and Prevention had declared tobacco "the single largest preventable cause of death and disability" in the United States. Yet for forty years, Congress had allowed the tobacco industry to operate with impunity. Since 1953, scientists had known that tobacco caused cancer in rats. But despite thousands of studies and overwhelming scientific consensus about its deadly effects, the industry's Washington lobby was so powerfully entrenched that tobacco effectively stood beyond the reach of the government to regulate or control.

In 1994 nearly twenty years had passed since I arrived in Washington as a young congressman from Los Angeles, and during that time I had seen firsthand how the tobacco industry manipulated Washington: how it spread enormous sums of money to both Republicans and Democrats; how it attempted to silence representatives of minority communities (whose members tobacco kills more quickly than the broader public) with lavish grants for local charities and arts programs; how it created the illusion of scientific authority by funding pseudoscientific outfits like the Council for Tobacco Research that *The Wall Street Journal* called "the hub of a massive effort to cast doubt on the links between smoking and disease"; and especially how the CEOs had shrewdly hidden themselves from view, instead putting forward these dubious "experts" and advertising icons like Joe Camel and the Newport Kids to serve as the public face of this deadly industry.

By inviting the CEOs to testify, I hoped to change that image and expose the men who controlled this deadly business to the full glare of the public spotlight. Many people had struggled for many years to lay the groundwork necessary for this day to happen.

Congress is held in low regard by much of the public, which tends to view its members as officious or inept. But most of the critics I encounter lack a full appreciation for what Congress really does. The Constitution confers powers on its members that, when properly deployed, can yield widespread benefits to all Americans. Tobacco is a good example. Over the years, my staff and I had done all we could to establish a public record of tobacco's harm and build what we hoped would become the necessary pressure to finally force government action. We had won some small skirmishes, narrowly passing legislation requiring warning labels on cigarettes and banning smoking on airplanes. In 1993, when the Environmental Protection Agency proved the deadly effect of secondhand smoke, I had introduced a bill banning smoking in public buildings, and then led a hearing in which the last six surgeons general—four Republicans and two Democrats—testified in support of it. Soon afterward, McDonald's announced plans to ban smoking in its restaurants, and so did the United States military.

Evidence had recently begun to leak from inside this notoriously secretive industry that companies were marketing to kids and spiking the level of nicotine in cigarettes to keep smokers addicted. This, too, had prompted a hearing just weeks before the CEOs had their turn. David Kessler, the commissioner of the Food and Drug Administration, had testified that cigarettes were "high-technology nicotine delivery systems," and he let it be known that the FDA was considering regulating tobacco, citing the reports of nicotine spiking as justification. Gradually but inexorably, my congressional allies and I had used the levers of government power to create national momentum to confront this vital issue.

All of this fed the growing awareness of tobacco's dangers. By April 1994, 91 percent of Americans believed that cigarettes were addictive. The tobacco industry, as it always did, used its considerable money and influence to strike back. In the months before the CEOs testified, the industry had sued the EPA for its report on secondhand smoke and the city of San Francisco for banning public smoking, and then it filed a $10 billion libel suit against ABC for its reports on nicotine spiking—all in an effort to intimidate and silence critics. What had finally compelled the CEOs to come out of the shadows and testify was the mounting pressure we had managed to create. Now, the full weight of the tobacco industry was about to strike at us.

THIS WAS A POSITION I WAS WELL ACCUSTOMED TO. NEARLY EVERY worthwhile fight in my career began with my being badly outmatched. The other guys always have more money. That's why Congress is so important. Run as it should be, it ensures that no special interest can ever be powerful enough to eclipse the public interest. The story of the tobacco fight, and many others like it, is testimony to how Congress can work for the greater good.

Sadly, the view of government as a positive force that serves its people is one that has all but vanished since I first ran for office. Today, disdain for government is so strong that it has given rise to the idea that Congress in particular cannot do much of anything right. This cynical outlook has been nurtured by a thirty-year-long crusade led by ideological conservatives to turn the American people against their elected officials by continually disparaging them and all that they do. Ronald Reagan epitomized this attitude when he declared, "The scariest words in the English language are, 'I'm from the government and I'm here to help.'"

As someone who has spent those thirty years in Congress working for the general good, I strongly reject this notion. I've lived the frustrations of Congress and spent a great deal of time investigating incompetent government, so I understand the complaints. But I also have plenty of experience passing legislation against fierce opposition, and then watching the bills bring important benefits to people all over the country. And I know firsthand how government oversight reduces fraud and abuse. Congress is far from perfect and would benefit from some important reforms—but at a fundamental level it not only works, it is a tremendous force for good.

I wrote this book to explain how Congress really works and to give an idea of the many accomplishments that are routinely overlooked, misunderstood, or drowned out by partisan attacks. During my time in Congress, I have participated in a number of difficult but important fights that have had enormous positive influence on people's lives—legislation limiting toxic air emissions, so we can all breathe cleaner air; expanding Medicaid coverage for the poor and elderly; banning smoking on airplanes; funding the first government-sponsored HIV/AIDS research; lowering drug prices through generic alternatives and fostering the development of hundreds of new drugs to treat rare diseases and conditions that pharmaceutical companies had ignored; putting nutritional labels on food, and keeping it free of pesticides, so that you know what you and your kids are eating; and establishing federal standards for nursing homes to protect the elderly from abuse and neglect. I have also used congressional oversight powers to protect taxpayer dollars and stop waste, fraud, and abuse in areas ranging from Wall Street to the Hurricane Katrina clean-up to the wars in Iraq and Afghanistan. In the chapters ahead, I'll use many of these examples to demonstrate why negative views of government are so often misguided and how the lessons of my three decades in the House of Representatives can be applied to make Congress even more effective.

ONE REASON PEOPLE DON'T APPRECIATE GOVERNMENT AS FULLY as they might is that many of the positive changes take years to fully materialize. Certainly, no one present at the tobacco hearings could have foreseen the magnitude of their effect. The iconic photograph of the seven CEOs standing with right hands raised as they swore an oath that each would proceed to break in full view of the American people did indeed change tobacco's public image; and their claim that they did not believe cigarettes to be addictive became national news. In the days after the hearing, the industry launched a massive counterattack against the "witch hunt" that it claimed its leaders had been forced to endure. One sympathetic columnist called the hearing "an odious, contemptible, puritanical display of arrogance and power," while another compared me to Joseph McCarthy. But they could not sustain the lie for very long. In the months and years that followed, key portions of the executives' testimony would collapse in the torrent of documents and testimony from industry insiders that the hearing unleashed. Even Hollywood took notice, as Russell Crowe and Al Pacino dramatized the story in the hit movie *The Insider*.

Driven by Congress, the focus on tobacco's dangers led states and municipalities across the country to ban smoking in public buildings, and persuaded untold numbers of people to quit smoking or, better, never to start. Countless lives were saved.

But on the morning of April 14, 1994, as I climbed the stairs to assume the chairman's seat, that was all still just a vague hope, and I could think only about the challenge at hand. Seated before me in the packed hearing room, flanked by television cameras, were the seven powerful men who together represented the American tobacco industry. The most formidable Washington lobby that money could buy sat just behind them, a phalanx of high-priced lawyers, political fixers, and public relations spinners who had managed to keep the industry shrouded in secrecy, and hold the government at bay, for almost forty years.

On my side sat a handful of committed colleagues whose years of hard work had culminated with this historic hearing in which each would play a key role. They included Mike Synar of Oklahoma, Ron Wyden of Oregon, and Mike Kreidler of Washington, who would describe in vivid detail to the tobacco executives seated across from him his own father's prolonged and terrible death from emphysema after a lifetime of smoking. My staff had locked themselves in the office the night before to develop lines of questioning and guarantee that nothing leaked to our resourceful foes. We had prepared well. But no one doubted that we were seriously outgunned.

In the moments before the proceedings got underway, I reminded myself how I had arrived here. I thought about my parents, who had instilled in me a belief that government matters and that public service is a noble calling; my early days in California politics, when I'd been part of a group of reformers that had overcome the state's entrenched powers; my battle sixteen years earlier against some of the most powerful men in Congress for the chairmanship of this very subcommittee, so that I might bring accountability to industries like tobacco that operate without any. Everything had built to this moment. This was why I was here.

Then I raised my right hand and banged down the gavel. "The meeting of the subcommittee will now come to order."

THE
WAXMAN
REPORT

CHAPTER 1

The Early Years

I WAS BORN IN 1939 IN THE EAST LOS ANGELES NEIGHBOR-hood of Boyle Heights. Though my parents met and married in Los Angeles, they share a common ancestry. Both families emigrated from what was then called the Bessarabia region of the Russian Empire (what is today known as Moldova), to escape the anti-Jewish pogrom of 1903. The Boyle Heights of my youth was a teeming immigrant community, with a heavy representation of Russian and Eastern European Jews, along with Mexicans, Japanese, and many others.

When I was growing up, politics was a passionate interest of the Waxman household. My father, Lou Waxman, was the most political person I knew, and my mother, Esther, was not far behind. One of my most vivid memories as a child is going to bed on the night of the 1948 election and waking up the next morning to find my parents still huddled around the radio listening to the news that Harry Truman had won.

My earliest lessons about politics were delivered over the dinner table. My father was an ardent Democrat, who worshipped Franklin Roosevelt and the New Deal. For a long time he worked for a retail grocery chain as a proud member of the Retail Clerks Union #770. Unions served the vital purpose of looking out for workers, he explained to me, because without their protection management would only hire clerks during the busy hours. The rest of the time you'd be out of a job, and unlikely to be able to support your family.

Like so many of his generation, my father was scarred by the Great Depression. The need to support his family forced him to quit high school, and he was never able to fulfill his dream of going to college. But his view of government, which he imparted to me, was unremittingly positive. He believed that it was a tremendous force for good and could do still more, often reminding me how much Roosevelt had done to help families like ours survive the hard times. It was the government, he would tell me, that finally stepped in to halt the practices of big business that had caused the Depression and got the country moving again. Business only looked out for its own. But government was the great equalizer. It ensured that the little guy had a chance.

One thing that has changed markedly since my childhood is how most Americans view their government. In Boyle Heights, everyone thought of government as an institution that helped people, an especially vital resource for the immigrant community. Government provided people with the means to get an education, through the public school system. It provided security for the elderly, through the Social Security program. It did not occur to anyone to rail against government or to regard it as a vast malign force, as so many people do today. To us, government supplied the means to move up the economic ladder and improve our lot in life. It provided a path to the middle class.

My family's passion for politics was as much active and participatory as ideological, and it manifested itself most prominently in the figure of my uncle, Al Waxman. My father's older brother was a fiery liberal, the founder and publisher of the local newspaper, the *East Side Journal*, whose proud Democratic viewpoint provided a sharp contrast and a necessary counterweight to what was then a very right-wing *Los Angeles Times*. During World War II, as Californians of Japanese heritage—many of them our neighbors—were rounded up and forced into camps, the *East Side Journal* was one of the few newspapers in the country to editorialize against this outrage.

Uncle Al's activist streak did not limit itself only to newsprint. Even back in the 1940s, Los Angeles was often blanketed by a thick layer of smog. No one knew precisely what caused this or quite how to fix it, so the Los Angeles County Smoke and Fumes Commission was established to investigate the problem, and as a figure of some prominence in the community, Uncle Al became one of its earliest appointees. He didn't last long. Soon after the commission began its inquiry into the reasons for the poor air quality, he concluded that pollution from local industry was a significant contributor. Nor was he shy about saying so. On a commission stacked with local bigwigs, blaming industry for the city's pollution caused a good deal of political discomfort for its members, and Al was soon pushed out. But his activism was always a source of family pride and his example offers a lesson that I have learned time and again during my career: Criticizing powerful interests is frequently necessary and does not make you a popular fellow.

AFTER WORLD WAR II, THE JEWISH COMMUNITY IN LOS ANGELES gravitated to the city's west side. The strip along Fairfax Avenue was soon bustling with delicatessens, Jewish stores, and kosher food outlets, serving, among many others, most of my family, along with many of our friends and neighbors. Hot to follow the action, Uncle Al sold the *East Side Journal* and established another newspaper, the *LA Reporter*, which was commonly re-

ferred to in the new neighborhood as "The Waxman Reporter."
After growing up in South Central Los Angeles, where we lived
above my father's grocery store, I moved west, too, enrolling
at the University of California–Los Angeles, where I decided to
study political science.

Besides satisfying my growing interest in politics, my choice
of major had the convenience of not requiring a heavy regimen
of classes, leaving plenty of time for extracurricular activities.
One of the first things I did at UCLA was to join the university's vibrant Young Democrats Club, where I soon developed
a close circle of friends. Many of those I knew and worked
with at that time—people like Phil and John Burton, Howard
and Michael Berman, Phil Isenberg, Willie Brown, and Dave
Roberti—would go on to remarkable political careers.

In those days, there was a lot of excitement among Democrats, particularly on college campuses in California. The
activist spirit that would explode in the 1960s was just beginning to stir. For committed liberals like my friends and myself,
the most important issues included a nuclear test ban treaty,
abolishing the notorious House Un-American Activities Committee, establishing diplomatic relations with Red China, and
championing civil rights legislation. Soon enough, opposition
to the escalating war in Vietnam became a central cause as
well. These positions were so outside the mainstream Democratic Party that, at one point, reporters asked John F. Kennedy
himself about the California Young Democrats. "I don't worry
much about those Young Democrats," he replied. "Time is on
our side." I suppose he meant that as we grew older, we would
come to see things his way. In fact, over time, people started to
see things our way.

The period around 1960 is remembered today for being
the time when John F. Kennedy captivated the nation. People
I meet still tell me that his example inspired them to get into

politics. His nomination at the 1960 Democratic convention, held in Los Angeles, was indeed significant. But at the time, we thought that if you considered yourself a true liberal, as we emphatically did, you had to be an Adlai Stevenson man. So my friends and I did what we could for the Stevenson cause.

As a newspaper publisher, Uncle Al commanded a pair of prized floor passes to the convention, which Howard Berman and I put to enterprising use. As soon as we entered the gallery, one of us would sneak back out with the passes. In this way we were eventually able to infiltrate all our friends to root for the "Draft Stevenson" movement—an effort that did not wind up succeeding, alas, although we did manage to make a lot of noise.

In the early 1960s, the California Democratic Party was divided into two factions. Atop one group, the traditional and somewhat more conservative Democrats, sat Jesse Unruh, the powerful speaker of the State Assembly. Atop the other, more liberal, group to which I belonged sat California's governor, Pat Brown. Unruh and Brown had a serious rivalry that also came to define the Young Democrats. There were Unruh people and Brown people, and for us liberals, wresting power from the Unruh faction that controlled the California Federation of Young Democrats was the constant struggle.

When I became the head of the federation's liberal caucus during my junior year in college, the task of outmaneuvering the Unruh crowd and taking control of the Young Democrats fell largely to me. The only way to do this, I recognized, was to out-organize the opposition. Organization is the bedrock of everything that happens in politics, the necessary precursor to any real change. So I began traveling around the state in the battered, two-tone, green-and-white Buick with large fins that was my primary means of transportation. I'd visit high schools and college campuses, to talk to Young Democrat clubs, appeal to their idealism, and try to make common cause with them and expand our numbers.

Control of the statewide federation of clubs was determined at an annual convention by whose candidate won the presidency. The first push to topple the Unruh folks that I participated in came in 1960, and though I spent a good deal of the academic year crisscrossing the state, our candidate came up short. Afterward, John Burton, Willie Brown, Howard Berman, and I sat despondent in a San Diego hotel room talking about what we'd do next. Phil Burton, several years older and by that time a California assemblyman, urged us to persevere. "You learn more by losing than you do by winning," he told us. Indeed, we had just learned that we much preferred winning.

Burton was already emerging as a force in national politics and would go on to exercise a tremendous influence on my career and on that of many others. He was very liberal, very smart, and very pragmatic. When serving in Congress in the 1970s, he came within a single vote of being elected House majority leader. His constant invocation was to perform the difficult work of organizing. He dismissed exalted types who only wanted to give speeches as "Manhattan Democratic liberals"—a real put-down in California. They always sounded great when they spoke, he complained, but they never managed to get anything done. This rang true to me. Burton believed that it was far more important to accomplish your political objectives than simply to say the right thing and draw cheers from the crowd. Only through the hard work of organization can you accomplish the toughest goals.

The following year all of us redoubled our efforts and I was back on the road. The federation's 1961 gathering buzzed with intrigue. We had worked furiously throughout the year to establish new clubs and add liberal members to those that already existed. It was clear to both sides that we were almost evenly matched. Every vote would count. Fights broke out before the credentials committee, delegates on both sides lobbied furiously, and still we were unsure of whether our candidate for president, Phil Isenberg, had the strength to prevail.

The vote came down to a single delegate, a fellow by the name of Richard Harmetz, the head of the Beverly Hills Young Democrats, who had arrived at the convention an Unruh supporter. An important lesson in politics is that you never know who your allies may turn out to be. Even adversaries can sometimes be persuaded to support your cause. When we suggested that Harmetz join our team and become a statewide officer, he shifted his loyalties and Isenberg prevailed. At long last the liberals took control of the Young Democrats.

MY FATHER NEVER LEFT ANY DOUBT THAT HE EXPECTED ME TO join the professional class. I had no mind for business and couldn't stand the sight of blood, which put medical school out of the question. So after college, I enrolled at the UCLA law school, convinced that a degree would be practical. But my primary interest continued to be the Young Democrats. With my faction now in control, we began pressing for the "far-out" issues we cared about. Looking back now, it's a little amusing to me that the ideas we championed were considered so radical. Everything from our support for civil rights and relations with China to our opposition to the Un-American Activities Committee and the Vietnam War had entered the mainstream of American politics or soon would. But back then we were still something of a spectacle.

In 1965, I won a two-year term as president of the California Federation of Young Democrats, a position of some visibility. Television talk shows were just beginning to take off, and as a leading Young Democrat I was often invited to appear as a guest. I suspect this had as much to do with what were considered to be my unorthodox views as my position in Democratic politics. I vividly recall one Los Angeles talk show where I found myself seated on a panel with a Kennedy-assassination conspiracy theorist and a woman who claimed to have been abducted by a UFO. Such was the novelty of my opposition to the Vietnam War and my criticism of Lyndon Johnson's prosecution of it—a president *of my own party*!—that the show's producers considered this an apt lineup.

But not everyone regarded my liberal cohorts and me as simply curiosities. The national Democratic Party's main power broker in California, a consigliere to both the Kennedy family and President Johnson, was a Los Angeles lawyer by the name of Eugene Wyman, who, much to my surprise, summoned me to a meeting shortly after I became president of CFYD. Wyman congratulated me on my new role, but was agitated about my opposition to the war, and he sought to impress upon me the need to tone down my criticism of the president. "You're in a position of authority when you speak for the Democratic Party," he complained. "You can't be a leader of the Democratic Party and be against this war and the president." I explained that I didn't think Johnson's policy in Vietnam was the right one. Wyman insisted that I couldn't say that. I was dumbfounded. "Well, how about civil rights?" I asked him. "Is it okay to talk about that?" "Oh, that would be fine," he replied. When our meeting ended, I left amused rather than intimidated that such an important man cared so much about what I had to say.

FOR ALL THAT I LOVED POLITICS, I NEVER ENVISIONED MYSELF RUNning for office. But in 1968, an opportunity arose that changed my mind. The longtime state assemblyman from our area, Lester McMillan, a local fixture at age seventy, was expected to retire. During his twenty-eight years in the assembly McMillan had compiled a solid liberal record, especially on civil rights.

Every year, he would offer a bill to eliminate the death penalty, which was a popular idea within his heavily liberal district. But on economic issues, McMillan had a reputation in Sacramento for being close to many of the "special interests." In 1965, he was indicted for bribery in a scandal connected to the construction of the Los Angeles Marina. He had stood trial, been acquitted, and afterward announced that he would run once more for reelection, in 1966, to clear his name. Then he would retire. At least, that was my assumption.

If McMillan quit, the seat would be wide open, and because the district was reliably liberal, winning the Democratic primary was tantamount to winning the general election. I figured there would be heavy competition, so the vote would likely be spread across many candidates. With my organizational skills and the support of the Waxman family newspaper, I thought my chances looked pretty good.

But there was one factor I hadn't reckoned on: Lester McMillan decided not to quit. When I went to see him, in the hopes of changing his mind, he did not seem particularly troubled by my challenge. "I have some advice for you," he told me. "Don't put your own money into the campaign."

As a close ally of Jesse Unruh's, McMillan had always won without much difficulty, and this year looked to be no different. In fact, there was reason to believe he might do better than ever. In 1968, Bobby Kennedy was running for president in the California primary, Unruh was heading the Kennedy campaign in California and McMillan was a Kennedy delegate—a truly significant factor in a district like McMillan's that was about one-third black, one-third Jewish, and one-third mixed ethnic. Kennedy was beloved in the black community, whose strong support McMillan had every right to expect.

I decided to run anyway, and rounded up my Young Democrat friends to help organize my campaign. Howard Berman's brother, Michael, a nineteen-year-old computer whiz at UC Berkeley, agreed to drop out and come down to Los Angeles to manage the campaign. Howard Elinson, a UCLA classmate who had become a professor of sociology, helped develop the message. The intersection of politics and technology barely existed in those days. But Michael Berman had an idea about how computers could help win an election. My cousin's husband, who worked in the computer industry, figured out with Michael that by punching in the information from local voter files they could write a program to generate individualized letters with messages targeted to different voter blocs and mail them to everyone in the district. Howard Elinson came up with distinct messages to appeal to the district's various ethnic and racial groups. And I spent months pounding the pavement, walking precincts, knocking on every door in every neighborhood to introduce myself to voters.

This exercise taught me that Lester McMillan might indeed be a renowned figure, but also that voters respond to personal contact. They appreciated that I was working to earn their votes and willing to listen to their concerns. After a while, I could tell that I was beginning to get through because people began to recognize me, even if not everyone was as well informed about the race as I would have liked. One morning, a woman came to the door with a broad smile of recognition. "There are only two people I'm voting for," she announced brightly. "You and Lester McMillan." I didn't have the heart to explain that we were opponents.

Another facet of the campaign did not proceed quite as smoothly. Family can be a big asset when you're running for office. Both my parents and my sister, Miriam, put in long hours at campaign headquarters. I was counting on the Waxman name to attract the Jewish vote and appeal to readers of the family newspaper, still informally called "The Waxman Reporter" even after Uncle Al died and my Aunt Ruth took over. The paper published influential front-page endorsements right before Election Day. So shortly after launching my campaign, I invited Aunt Ruth to lunch to discuss my candidacy and what I assumed would be her eager support. Instead, looking somewhat pained, she delivered some unexpected news. "I'm endorsing Lester McMillan," she told me. The *LA Reporter* had supported McMillan for years, and he'd been a friend of my uncle's: Despite family ties, Aunt Ruth did not think it proper to abandon him. As a consolation, she offered me a weekly column to make the case for my candidacy to her readers. Figuring that guilt would get the better of her long before Election Day, I accepted the offer and made a breakfast date for the following week to try again. This became a weekly ritual—and, in the end, not a successful one. Aunt Ruth remained true to her word and endorsed Lester McMillan on Election Day (though I'm pleased to report that we remained very close, and that she has endorsed me ever since).

Oddly enough, my most helpful endorsement was entirely unsolicited. One day, a long, black, chauffeur-driven limousine pulled up to the curb in front of my campaign headquarters, and an elegantly dressed older African-American man stepped out, gazed up at the "WAXMAN FOR STATE ASSEMBLY" billboard above the door, and, though he was frail and used a cane, pushed his way inside. "I saw the name Waxman and I wasn't sure who it was," he said to me. When I introduced myself and explained that my family had lived in the community for years, he smiled and nodded. His name was Colonel Leon Washington and he turned out to be the publisher of the local black newspaper, the *Los Angeles Sentinel*. He remembered Uncle Al because the *Sentinel* and the *East Side Journal* had been the only two liberal newspapers in town. After we'd chatted for a while, he said, "I'm going to support you." I'm ashamed to admit that I waited for him to ask something in return, imagining that he'd want me to buy advertising in the *Sentinel*. But all that he asked was that, if elected, would I please see to it that a post office opened in the black neighborhood, which didn't have one.

Lester McMillan never took me seriously, so he didn't put on much of a campaign. In the black neighborhoods, where his status as a Bobby Kennedy delegate should have earned him huge margins, he did nothing at all. Meanwhile, I had spent months knocking on doors and developed a slate piece—a voter guide—with Berman and Elinson urging people to vote for "Waxman and Kennedy." As the June primary neared, we received word that Kennedy himself would appear at a political rally along Fairfax Avenue. On the day of the rally, the street was closed off. One of my campaign workers got hold of a loudspeaker. "Come to Fairfax to hear Senator Kennedy and meet Assembly candidate Henry Waxman!" blared the message. When Kennedy finally arrived, he waved for only a few moments before driving off.

It hardly mattered. On Election Day, I wound up beating McMillan by a margin of two to one. To my surprise, I performed even better in the black neighborhoods than in the Jewish ones. (Today, the Colonel Leon H. Washington Jr. Post Office sits at 43rd Street and Central Avenue in Los Angeles.)

But the celebration of my first great political victory was short-lived. As friends and family gathered to cheer at campaign headquarters, stunning news was broadcast on the television set: Bobby Kennedy had been shot across town.

The Art
of
Making Laws

CHAPTER 2

California State Assembly to Congressional Subcommittee Chairman

POLITICAL PARTIES IN CALIFORNIA HAVE TRADITIONALLY been weak, a consequence of the early twentieth-century Progressives, like the state's formidable governor and senator Hiram Johnson, who were suspicious of them and worked to limit their influence. The absence of a strong party organization meant that there was no "machine" to dole out desirable appointments and committee assignments or to handpick candidates and mediate their disputes. In 1960s Sacramento the consequence of these conditions was to concentrate power in the legendary speaker of the State Assembly, Jesse Unruh.

Unruh's political views were often quite liberal. In 1959, Unruh, a lapsed Mennonite, authored California's Civil Rights Act, which outlawed racial discrimination in housing and employment and became a model for later reforms. But more than any policy, his overriding obsession was wielding power, and during his career he created a top-down system in which most of what happened in the Assembly flowed directly from the speaker.

Emblematic of Unruh's command over the legislature was a famous story that involved an Oakland assemblyman named Bob Crown, who had been an ally of the speaker's, but had broken with him by the time I arrived. Crown was universally regarded as a shrewd operator and a felicitous speaker, so during the time when they were aligned, he often carried Unruh's bills in the Assembly. One day in a committee hearing, Crown was wrapping up a speech that carefully laid out the arguments against the pending measure when one of Unruh's lackeys appeared in the back of the room and began frantically signaling to him that the speaker in fact wished for the bill to pass. Without missing a beat, Crown declared "And that's what opponents of this legislation would claim about this bill" before proceeding to deliver an equally impassioned statement of support. When I got to Sacramento, Crown befriended me and helped illuminate the Assembly's many strange byways of power. To this eager novice, he explained how the world worked.

Unruh's power derived from his control over legislators. Lacking a strong party organization to help a legislator facing a tough race, it was Unruh's ability, and nobody else's, to help those loyal to him with money and choice committee assignments. As such, he was often hostile to the "outsider" liberal reformers elected to office in the 1960s and set on changing the old ways. Unruh thought the old ways worked just fine. His famous remark about lobbyists gives a good sense of his outsize personality, and of how things were when I arrived in the State Assembly: "If you can't take their money, drink their booze, screw their women, and then come in here the next day and vote against them, you don't belong in Sacramento."

The great struggle between Jesse Unruh and Pat Brown had

ended just before I arrived in Sacramento. Ronald Reagan had defeated Brown in the 1966 gubernatorial election. And though I won an Assembly seat in 1968, my party hadn't fared remotely so well: The Republicans gained a majority, relegating Unruh to an unaccustomed place in the minority. Suddenly, Democrats found themselves united on recovering a majority.

Unruh was no slouch at organizing. He and his allies had long taken money from the special interests to fund the campaigns that kept them in power. At his say-so, Democrats in safe seats would often raise money for colleagues facing tough races in order to maximize the party's strength—a smart strategy. It wasn't enough to keep the Republicans at bay in 1968. But a new generation of liberals that included many of my fellow Young Democrats—John Burton, Willie Brown, Dave Roberti, and Bob Moretti, to name just a few—had begun winning Assembly seats, and brought with them new methods of organizing that they now deployed on behalf of the broader party. The computerized targeting that my campaign pioneered was one such technique, and it earned me a central role in our counterattack.

Late 1960s Sacramento had a distinctive political culture. It was a capital in the middle of nowhere, so legislators tended to go up for the week and return home on weekends. A legislator's Sacramento social life consisted mainly of raucous parties. (If nothing else, Jesse Unruh's political philosophy put a premium on conviviality.) Because so many of the men brought their girlfriends to these parties, wives were not welcome. The social pressure was strong enough that when I met my wife, Janet, during my time in Sacramento, I had to break the news that I could bring her to some of these gatherings—but only until we were married.

Perhaps not surprisingly, when it came to committee assignments, most legislators scrambled for seats on what were

known as the "juice committees"—those responsible for overseeing the special interest groups that lavished the most desired forms of attention on lawmakers. One such committee
dealt with racetracks; another oversaw liquor sales. Seats on
the juice committees were a sought-after plum; chairing one
guaranteed that you would be feted like a Roman nobleman.
Several of my colleagues seemed to orient their entire careers
toward realizing this distinction.

AS SOMEONE WHO WAS LOW-KEY BUT HIGHLY POLITICAL, I WAS
more than satisfied to chair the Elections and Redistricting
Committee, and hired Michael Berman to be my right-hand
man. With Unruh planning to challenge Reagan for the gover-
norship in 1970, my friend Bob Moretti was angling to become
the next Democratic speaker, and I was set on doing everything I could to help him. He turned to me to ensure that our
party would be in the best possible position to win and hold on
to a majority after the decennial round of redistricting.

Political redistricting is one of those obscure backroom exer-
cises whose particulars can be dry and difficult to understand,
but carry great weight in the stakes of power. Every ten years,
in statehouses across the country, the geographic boundaries
of congressional districts are redrawn ("redistricted") to reflect
the latest demographic information from the United States
Census. If a state's population increases, as it usually does in
California, the state might be awarded additional congressional
seats. If it has declined, seats can be taken away. Either shift
sets off a mad scramble—driven by ambition, party loyalty, and
raw self-interest—to craft new districts. In California, the party
that controls the state legislature gets to redraw the map.

Democrats were fortunate enough to win back a narrow
majority in the State Assembly in 1970, the year in which the
new census data were released. Bob Moretti became the new

speaker. My job was to consult with Phil Burton, a master of re-districting now serving in Congress, to figure out how to draw a map that would yield the best result for the Democratic Party. It was a lot of work, but I was confident we'd get it done well before the end of the summer. So Janet and I planned our wedding for October.

In theory, redistricting should be a simple exercise: Fiddle with the borders until you've maximized the number of safe Democratic seats and call it a day. In practice, I was soon to discover, the task demands an advanced degree in psychology, a tireless capacity for salesmanship, and the patience of Job.

Redistricting brings out the best and worst in politicians. Although an admirable few agree to whatever map best serves their party's interests, many more beg and plead for what seem the strangest of reasons. Say a district is redrawn in such a way that it maintains a member's core constituency and adds a few more Democratic neighborhoods. Surely an easy sell. But you never know how the incumbent will react. "Oh, but my brother-in-law lives over here—I can't *possibly* give up that neighborhood!" "Don't you dare chop off the western edge of my district—my biggest donor lives there!" "Please, Henry, give me more Republicans if you must, but put my mother-in-law in the next district over!"

And, of course, when you have as narrow a margin as we Democrats did that year—42-38—anyone can hold up the process. At the same time my Democratic colleagues were wheedling for geographic favors, my Republican counterpart, Jerry Lewis, who later became a colleague in Congress, was doing all that he could to protect his own party's incumbents. Redistricting always labors under the threat that if the minority party is sufficiently aggrieved by the map, they can go to court or, if the governor is a member of the party, have him veto the bill. The negotiations dragged on, and my wedding date loomed ever closer. In late summer, it looked briefly as though we might strike a deal. But a special election held in August flipped a seat to the Republicans, further narrowing the margin. Janet and I decided we had better go ahead with the wedding.

When the big day arrived, no deal had been reached, though one did appear tantalizingly close. Many of my colleagues attended the wedding. As the new Mr. and Mrs. Waxman greeted the receiving line, I spotted our brand-new Speaker Moretti looking preoccupied. When he reached Janet and me, he congratulated us and then leaned in close to whisper. "Look, Henry," he said, "I know it's your wedding, but a couple of the guys coming down the line haven't committed to the bill yet . . ." As the recalcitrant assemblymen made their way down the line to offer their blessings, I thanked each of them and then added, "Now, I sure hope I can count on your support for the redistricting bill."

That fall it finally passed—and Governor Reagan promptly vetoed it. We appealed in vain to the California Supreme Court. The law states that "the governor must sign the bill" and Reagan refused, wagering that a court-mandated plan would better serve Republican interests than did ours. The court called for a new map for 1974 and used the old districts for 1972. Two years' hard work amounted to a do-over.

THANKFULLY, MY ASSEMBLY WORK WAS NOT LIMITED TO REDIS-tricting. Early on, I decided that in order to become an effective legislator I should develop an area of expertise, which would enable me to exert outsized influence whenever that subject arose. Because my district was home to a large elderly population, health policy struck me as a good specialization. People always need good health care and it is an area where government has historically had a hugely beneficial effect: providing access to care, supporting research to prevent and cure diseases, and overseeing the system to end abuses and ensure efficient function. In 1968, health policy was also an excitingly new frontier. Congress had recently created the federal Medicare and Medicaid programs, and making sure that they were properly implemented was among the most important services a legislator could provide his constituents.

Since this was the furthest thing from a juice assignment, the speaker was happy to appoint me to the Assembly Health Committee. In order to learn the ins and outs of policy, I began consulting doctors, hospital administrators, constituents, and anyone else I thought might have something to teach me. Lobbyists, too, are always eager to "educate" legislators on their pet issues, at least from the point of view they were paid to push. To avoid being hypnotized by their arguments, I also subscribed to physicians magazines to learn what issues doctors were concerned about and to see if there was a way that I might be able to help.

When my first legislative session began in 1969, Ronald Reagan had targeted Medi-Cal (as California's Medicaid program is known). As a conservative, Reagan was eager to shrink the size of government, and intended to cut a significant number of people from the program and reduce payments to doctors who treated Medi-Cal patients. Both actions would lower the cost—though with the obvious negative effects of leaving many people uninsured and diminishing the number of doctors willing to treat those still covered.

The health committee held hearings on Reagan's proposals to illustrate the likely consequences of his cuts. In addition to garnering public attention, this prompted the California Rural Legal Assistance to file suit to halt them, on the grounds that Reagan did not have the right to take away people's health care by removing them from Medi-Cal, an argument the court upheld.

During the next legislative session, after I declined the redistricting job and became chairman of the Health Committee instead, Reagan tried again. Constituents and public interest groups had been complaining to me that some state-licensed Medi-Cal plans were run by operators who did not have the contracts with doctors and hospitals that they claimed in order to get government funding, and thus could not provide access to the care that patients needed. People duped into enrolling in bad plans discovered that they couldn't get out of them.

Having been prevented from kicking Medi-Cal recipients out of the program, Reagan next tried to move patients from private doctors to health maintenance organizations, or HMOs, as a way of limiting costs. Medi-Cal paid the bills of Californians who chose to visit their own doctors. Reagan wanted to move them into HMOs in order to cap the amount of money the state had to pay. My father's union had offered membership in Kaiser Permanente's HMO, so I had always looked favorably upon the concept and believed that HMOs provided a model for the future of health care. But the system Reagan presided over was badly flawed. Though patients in Medi-Cal HMOs cost the state less than those going to private doctors, many of these plans did not have doctors or other medical personnel to see people when care was needed.

Instead of removing people from Medi-Cal, Reagan had state workers go door to door in poor neighborhoods tricking people into "voluntarily" signing up for HMOs. Sometimes these workers dressed as doctors and frightened people by saying that they had to switch over to the HMO or they'd lose their health care. This created a terrible situation. Many of the people who signed up for the plan did not understand what it was and wound up being turned away by their old doctors. This left a sick and vulnerable population confused and unable to get the health care to which they were legally entitled.

As chairman of the Health Committee, I held oversight hearings to dramatize many of the abuses being inflicted at Reagan's behest, and we set to work writing legislation to halt them. In 1972, a Republican colleague and I authored the Waxman-Duffy Act, which set standards for HMOs that included public hearings to establish that anyone seeking a government Medi-Cal contract had the necessary financial resources and service providers to deliver quality care to his patients. Seeing how the combination of oversight hearings and legislation could improve the lives of so many people further persuaded me of what government can do for its people.

NOW THAT I WAS MARRIED, I DECIDED THAT MY OWN LIFE WITH Janet and my stepdaughter, Carol, needed a little more grounding. The life of a legislator can be an oddly transient one. Because district borders can shift so easily, I'd always held off on buying a house. But feeling that my Assembly seat was more or less secure, we decided it was time to find a home for our family.

When we were first married, Janet had spotted a house that she loved in Sacramento. Serendipitously, it appeared on the market right around the time we decided to settle down. She went for a tour and returned declaring that she had indeed found our dream house. So we bought it.

After the legislature and governor failed to pass a redistricting law for 1974, the court appointed an independent "master" to draw the lines. On the same day in 1974 that we moved into our new Sacramento house, the California Supreme Court released its redistricting map, which made it clear that I'd win my next Assembly race easily. It was also clear that I had a safe path to the local State Senate seat if I wanted to go that route. But another possibility was even more tantalizing: A brand-new congressional district had been drawn in the area and therefore lacked an incumbent.

Janet and I discussed the options and quickly agreed on our next move. "Let's do Congress," she told me. "I won't unpack." As fast as we'd bought it, we turned around and sold our dream house and moved back to Los Angeles to prepare for my next campaign.

People tend to assume that the most difficult part of a political race is facing off against the others who have chosen to run. But often the key to winning is convincing potential opponents not to run in the first place. That was the task before me as I plotted my 1974 congressional campaign. The new district was so safely Democratic that my main job was to persuade fellow Democrats not to run against me. `

In order to show strength, I began by collecting the endorsements of as many public officials and community leaders as I could in the hope of discouraging potential challengers. The most imposing looked to be a city councilman named Ed Edelman, who was already running for the position of Los Angeles county supervisor. I went to visit him and proposed that we support each other: I'd endorse him for supervisor and he, in turn, would endorse me for Congress. Edelman was clearly tempted by the bigger prize, but he'd already embarked on one race that my endorsement would make a little easier to win, and after weighing his options, he agreed. Our plan worked. That fall, I was elected to the U.S. House of Representatives from California's 24th District without even facing significant competition.

THE UNITED STATES CONGRESS "CLASS OF 1974" WAS A HISTORIC one because it was the first elected in the wake of Watergate. Ninety-two new representatives, most of them Democrats like me, swept into the House of Representatives bearing a message of reform. Though Watergate had played almost no role at all in my own race, I shared the eagerness for change and the desire to take on the entrenched powers and clean up Washington.

When I arrived in Congress, the reform movement already could be thought of as manifesting on two fronts. The first was within the Congress itself, as a younger generation tried to dismantle the antiquated seniority system. From around the turn of the century, congressional rank had been determined solely by a member's length of service. This meant that the most powerful legislators were simply the ones who had been around longest. They chaired the most important committees, and their power was nearly absolute. A chairman could create and abolish subcommittees, name the subcommittee chairmen (taking the role for himself if he wished), and determine when to hold hearings. The chairmen also controlled the entire committee staff.

The seniority system produced the handful of famous Southern Democrats who had long dominated the Congress when I arrived. Nowhere were the system's shortcomings better illustrated than in Howard "Judge" Smith of Virginia, chairman of the House Rules Committee, who had managed to block civil rights legislation for years by refusing to allow bills to go to the floor for a vote. When the Civil Rights Act of 1957 came before his committee, Smith famously declared, "The Southern people have never accepted the colored race as a race of people who had equal intelligence and education and social attainment as the white people of the South." It took reformers five years to change the rules sufficiently for the Civil Rights Act to make it to the House floor.

Behavior like Judge Smith's so disgraced the old system that challenges finally became possible. In 1971, members passed a resolution stipulating that seniority would no longer be the sole criterion for chairmanships and established voting procedures for the removal of chairmen. In 1973, the first such votes were held, though they were little more than formalities, and every chairman survived. In 1975, the influx of change-minded members that I was among provided the impetus to finally topple a few of the old lions: Wright Patman of the Banking Committee, F. Edward Hebert of the Armed Services Committee, and W. R. Poage of the Agriculture Committee.

What was overtaking Congress in the 1970s was a lot like what had occurred in the California Assembly in the 1960s. A new generation was fighting to change the old way of doing things—and now, as then, the man at the center of the action was my friend Phil Burton. Burton was the chairman of the Democratic Caucus, and like many reformers of the day set on shifting the balance of power from the chairmen to the caucus members. Burton wanted the chairmen to feel that they were accountable, not just to themselves but to the other Democratic members of the House. The unexpected defeat of three committee chairs in 1975 conveyed the message loud and clear.

The other major component of reform in Washington when I arrived was the mounting opposition to the concentration of power in the executive branch, a direct response to the problems of Watergate and Richard Nixon's "Imperial Presidency." As the Watergate scandal unfolded in the pages of *The Washington Post*, readers learned that the infamous break-in was merely the tip of the iceberg. The Nixon administration had spied on private citizens, used the Internal Revenue Service against political enemies, and routinely lied to and misled Congress and the American people.

Congress acquitted itself ably in its response to Watergate. On the legislative front, campaign finance reform established a new set of laws aimed at curbing the influence of money on elections, while the Freedom of Information Act encouraged government openness. Spurred by the *Post* stories, House and Senate oversight hearings enabled congressional investigators to dig deeply enough to bring all the facts to light and expose the full extent of the Watergate scandal. Congressmen and senators of both parties routinely stood up to the White House. And it was the House of Representatives that finally impeached the president and brought about his resignation.

The public's view of Congress during Watergate was generally favorable. But I believe that the combination of two events that originated in the executive branch—Watergate and the Vietnam War—led to such widespread disillusionment with government that the American people eventually lost faith in the Congress as well.

IN THE MIDST OF THESE HISTORIC CHANGES, IT REMAINED FOR ME to figure out the day-to-day business of the Congress. My interest in health care led me to pursue a seat on the Energy and Commerce Committee, which has legislative jurisdiction over most health issues. Along with the Ways and Means Committee, Energy and Commerce is one of the two "power" committees in the House, because both have enormous responsibilities that encompass much of the American economy. Along with a handful of my freshman classmates, I got my desired assignment to Energy and Commerce, and when we drew straws to determine seniority, I came out on top.

As if by script, we were immediately plunged into a battle over the chairmanship of the Oversight Subcommittee that pitted Harley Staggers, a West Virginian who chaired the full committee, against John Moss, a reform-minded challenger from Sacramento. As a new member, I was courted vigorously by both sides and familiar with neither. Staggers, in his West Virginia drawl, told me, "I want to do what's best for America, and I'm a good Christian." It seemed a rather strange appeal for my vote. Moss's entreaty was that he was in tune with the new generation and all that it stood for. When the time came for members to cast their secret ballots, most of my class and I sided with Moss, who prevailed.

Moss went on to become one of the great masters of the oversight process, and it was through his example that I first learned how it was done. He not only held hearings to highlight problems and abuses, but did so in ways designed to redound to his party's electoral benefit. There is a tendency, even among elected officials, to think of a congressman's various responsibilities—campaigning, fund-raising, legislating—as discrete enterprises. In reality, they're closely connected. Moss demonstrated this by using his oversight power to spotlight many of the themes that would become critical issues in the 1976 election. These included the Republican Party's countless abuses of power, but also such seemingly unconnected things as the Arab boycott of Israel.

In 1975, President Gerald Ford had said of the boycott, "Such discrimination is totally contrary to the American tradition and repugnant to American values." Moss held a hearing in which he revealed that Ford's own Commerce Department had solicited U.S. businesses on behalf of Arab nations that required them to boycott Israel. Moss knew that U.S. law required companies to notify the Commerce Department of requests to comply with the boycott and also whether or not the company did so. He invited Commerce Secretary Rogers Morton to testify and asked him to release the list of U.S. companies. Morton refused, effectively putting the Republican Party on the side of the Arabs. A public uproar ensued, and Moss initiated contempt proceedings against Morton, who finally yielded. In a presidential debate with Ford several months later, Jimmy Carter invoked the Arab boycott and vowed to outlaw any cooperation in a Carter administration.

Because the pace of legislation is slow and complicated and the process itself arcane, Congress is often difficult for the media to cover, especially television. But an oversight hearing, particularly on a highly charged issue, is an exception to this rule: Run properly, it has a clear story line, compelling characters, and frequent dramatic clashes. Furthermore, congressmen routinely tailor their presentations for television by using visual props and colorful sound bites. Moss had a keen awareness of this, and was even more effective because he generously allowed others to take the lead in questioning witnesses. His oversight hearings frequently made the evening news on all three major television networks.

I learned from Moss that oversight hearings were a golden opportunity to bring public attention to an issue, which instantly made it a higher priority for Congress. The practical effect of a successful hearing is that the media will immediately want to know three things: How did this happen? Whose fault is it? Why isn't it being stopped? The ensuing pressure often forces the responsible party to take action or creates an imperative for legislation.

The other important figure I encountered on the Energy and Commerce Committee was Paul Rogers, a moderate Democrat from West Palm Beach, Florida, whose father, Dwight Rogers, had preceded him in Congress. Paul Rogers was the chairman of the Subcommittee on Health and the Environment when I joined in 1975, though he was best known for his nickname, "Mr. Health." During his twenty-four-year career, he helped draft and pass such important legislation as the National Cancer Act, the Clean Air Act, and the Emergency Medical Services Act, among many others. But his skill as a chairman was what influenced me the most.

Having come from the top-down world of the California Assembly, I was astonished to see how Rogers ran committee meetings. Though a Democrat, he operated as though party affiliation did not exist, soliciting input as readily from Republicans as Democrats. When a bill was being considered by the subcommittee, he would walk us through it, section by section, allowing those members with specialized expertise to explain the importance of various issues and lead bipartisan discussions on what changes or amendments might improve them. Rogers always tried to reach consensus between Republicans and Democrats on how a bill would be modeled and what it should say. To my amazement, I learned that I—a mere freshman!—could influence a bill by speaking up and making a good point, which would shift the consensus in my direction. This was completely unlike the way Jesse Unruh had run the Assembly.

The genius of Rogers's method was manifold. Because everyone's views were considered, we all felt invested in the bill, even if it did not end up going our way. Because bills were never rammed through on party-line votes, Rogers could frequently put together different coalitions of Republicans and Democrats, which made it much harder for special interests to influence the process and much easier for us to pass good legislation. But most of all, the idea that a subcommittee possessed genuine expertise and that its decisions and legislation merited respect and deference from the full committee was widely accepted. During a House floor vote, for instance, it was common to hear members of both parties say, "The committee wants an 'aye' vote on the amendment" or "The committee wants a 'no' vote," because everyone respected the power of the committees. Rather than a top-down system, the congressional process when I arrived was bottom-up, with benefits that were clear to everyone.

IN 1979, PAUL ROGERS SURPRISED EVERYONE BY ANNOUNCING HIS retirement. I had been in Congress for four years, and two Democrats senior to me appeared likely to bid for his chairmanship. The first opted not to. But the second, Richardson Preyer, decided to run. Preyer was a respected moderate from North Carolina, the very embodiment of an enlightened Southern Democrat. He was distinguished, honorable (he had been a judge), and staunchly for civil rights. But hailing from tobacco country, he didn't think cigarettes were a health problem, as I did. And as a wealthy man whose family fortune derived from the Richardson-Merrill Pharmaceutical Company, makers of Vicks VapoRub, his becoming chairman presented a serious conflict of interest. One of the subcommittee's major functions is overseeing the Food and Drug Administration.

My own view was that the caucus ought to select the best person for the job. I'd been active on the subcommittee and believed I knew more about health policy than most of my colleagues. And I cared deeply about health and the environment—it was one of the main reasons I'd run for Congress. So I decided to challenge him.

Despite a few cracks in the facade, the seniority system very much still held sway. The older generation, including such legendary liberal reformers as Dick Bolling, reacted angrily to my perceived impertinence. But I was not without support. The environmental, consumer, and labor groups all lined up behind me. And a kind of generational solidarity among the younger, reform-minded members took hold to counter the old guard. I focused my attention on a dozen or so of my subcommittee colleagues whose votes would determine my fate.

Congressmen choose their leaders for all sorts of reasons: friendship, substance, ambition, money, regional and generational loyalties, and sometimes, I suspect, simply on a whim. A successful politician must work creatively until he finds the right claim on his colleagues' support. After I'd spoken with each of the undecideds, I tried to figure out who else I could contact to persuade to go my way. Tim Wirth of Colorado was a serious environmentalist. A number of my Los Angeles supporters agreed to lobby him on my behalf. Bob Eckhardt, a Houston liberal, was concerned about the influence of pharmaceutical companies. But I always suspected that he ultimately yielded not to my entreaties but to his daughter's wish that he support me. Someone else I'd worked closely with, but who represented a Southern tobacco state, was Al Gore. Difficult as it must have been not to support a fellow Southern moderate, Gore, who was a personal friend, cared a great deal about the dangers of tobacco and the conflicts a Preyer chairmanship would pose. In the end, he cast a very brave vote for me.

Preyer's allies did not roll over. Their main line of attack was to claim that I was attempting to buy the chairmanship by donating money from a political action committee to my fellow members. In California, giving money to one's colleagues was standard practice and, more to the point, smart politics—Jesse Unruh built and maintained a Democratic majority by seeing that his legislators had the means to get reelected.

I brought this practice with me to Congress because it yields important political benefits. As with oversight hearings, the tendency is always to look at the issue of money in isolation—in fact, because the influence of money in politics is such a fraught subject, the tendency is probably stronger here than anywhere else. The widespread view of money's role in politics is simply that it's bad. But rather than think of it as "good" or "bad," it's more useful to think of money as a political fact of life, and to develop a realist's understanding of how it flows and influences the business of Washington. Money is as important to the substantive work of Congress as a bill or an election. Everything intertwines.

To pass good legislation, you must first be surrounded by the right kind of people. When you find like-minded colleagues, you want to help in whatever way you can to make sure they

stay put. Having a good committee lineup broadens the possi-
bilities of what can be achieved (just as a bad one limits them).
This is one reason why I spend so much time and effort trying
to influence who gets on my committee. Before you can move
legislation, you must first lay the groundwork by making sure
that the right pieces are in place. It's like chess. A single vote
can be the difference between a strong acid rain provision and
a weak one.

The luxury of a safe seat meant that I didn't need to raise
much money for my own reelection. Instead, from the time
I arrived in Congress, I donated to those whom I considered
valuable allies. Though it displeased some traditionalists,
this practice has had positive results. Year after year, many
of the members I supported have cast key votes on important legislation.

But when I went up against Preyer, this approach was bit-
terly disputed. Dick Bolling declared himself so offended that
I had given money to people on the committee as to suggest
that I be stripped of my seniority. *The New York Times* edito-
rial page sided with my critics. At the time, the idea of being
criticized for helping my fellow Democrats get reelected upset
me. But I came to realize that the institution of Congress was
changing, and that was sometimes wrenching for the young
and the old alike.

I tried to focus on the immediate task by having lunch with
every member of the committee to make my pitch personally.
Some I went back to again and again. The work of a congressman involves a lot of process, and it is often far from glamor-
ous. But experience had taught me that persistent effort pays
off.

So far as I could tell, Richardson Preyer did not campaign
very hard. Though courtly and well liked, he was also a bit dif-
fident. Accustomed to the culture of seniority, he seemed to

find the idea of politicking for a chairmanship ever so slightly demeaning, and so he would not deign to ask for votes.

Under House rules, a subcommittee chairman is not chosen in a head-to-head race. Instead, the senior member must bid for it and either be elected or defeated. When at last the day arrived, the voting went 16-14 against Preyer. In the next round of voting moments later, I became chairman of Health and Environment, and the great changes underway in Congress took another turn. It was the first time in the history of the institution that someone had won a subcommittee chairmanship out of the line of seniority.

CHAPTER 3

HIV/AIDS and the Ryan White Act

AS THE NEW CHAIRMAN OF THE HOUSE SUBCOMMITTEE on Health and the Environment, I did not expect to be plunged immediately into a serious public health crisis. But that is exactly what happened when the AIDS epidemic struck in 1981. The story of this epidemic illustrates how Congress is capable of both heroic actions and astonishingly damaging ones—often on the same issue—and how, in this case, lawmakers and public health officials persevered to pass the first major federal legislation dealing with the AIDS crisis, the Ryan White CARE Act.

One advantage of being a committee chairman is the additional staff who come with the job. I've always believed that a congressman's responsibilities, beyond processing legislation, include staying attuned to important issues confronting other parts of the government. Staffers are invaluable in this regard, because by circulating through the agencies they can vastly expand a congressman's range of knowledge. This is how I first learned about AIDS.

In early 1981, the "Reagan Revolution" had just gotten underway, and the new president was bent upon slashing domestic spending. His primary enforcer was David Stockman, a bespectacled math whiz who headed the Office of Management and Budget. Stockman pored over the federal budget looking for programs to cut, and recorded each one that he found in a ledger that everybody referred to as "The Stockman Black Book." A member of my committee staff, Tim Westmoreland, returned from a visit to the Centers for Disease Control in Atlanta to report that the Stockman Black Book was causing serious concern. Public health agencies like the Centers for Disease Control (CDC), the National Institutes of Health (NIH), and the Food and Drug Administration (FDA) all do tremendous work, and having staffers who know what they're up to gives us an idea of what's coming down the pike and how we might help. Reagan proposed massive cuts to health programs, and CDC scientists were alarmed about the potential effects. "There's going to be a disaster," Tim reported to me. "It could be an FDA disaster, an NIH disaster, or a CDC disaster, but if these agencies get cut something has got to give." So in the summer of 1981, the Stockman Black Book had us all bracing for an epidemic—but we imagined that it would strike in the area of preventable childhood illnesses, since Reagan effectively wanted to cut the immunization budget in half.

I worried enough about this to hold a hearing on the proposed cuts, and brought in a Nobel laureate, the co-developer of the polio vaccine, to describe the public health crisis that could result. With the eventual help of Pete Domenici, a Republican senator from New Mexico, we protected the immunization program.

An epidemic came anyway. While Tim was in Atlanta learning about immunizations, a CDC scientist had suggested that he meet with a colleague named Jim Curran, who was described as "a VD doctor." Curran had noticed an outbreak of a strange and deadly pneumonia that was showing up in gay men in Los Angeles, specifically in West Hollywood, which is part of my district. Today, Jim Curran is widely recognized as a hero in the struggle against AIDS, a Sherlock Holmes who first spotted the disease and raised the alarm among epidemiologists. In the summer of 1981, however, he was still making inroads into a community fearful of government (homosexuality was still a felony in many states) and not yet ravaged by the nameless and invisible disease that was already expanding geometrically and invisibly among its members. He turned down our offer of a congressional hearing to highlight the need for research money in this new area, fearing that the attention would hamper his efforts. But he promised to stay in touch. "I'll call you when I'm ready," he told us. The following January, Curran was ready. Feeling he had built sufficient trust in the gay community to move forward, he said, "I think we can withstand this." Soon after, we convened what is known as a field hearing at the Gay and Lesbian Community Services Center in Los Angeles, where Curran and other leading health officials provided testimony. On that day in April 1982, a single reporter, from the *Los Angeles Times*, showed up to cover the first congressional hearing on the AIDS crisis.

THE BEST WAY FOR CONGRESS TO HANDLE AN EMERGING EPIDEMIC is to begin by drawing attention to it. The next step is to provide money for research. Later on, when more information is available, the focus can shift to prevention and treatment. Each of these steps was made more difficult, and the public health consequences more dire, because Republicans in Congress and in the Reagan administration cast AIDS as a "gay disease."

Much of what a chairman can do depends on the minority members of the committee, his counterparts across the aisle.

In the 1980s, the ranking member was a thoughtful and decent Republican from Illinois named Ed Madigan, with whom I worked successfully on many occasions. But Madigan had to contend with Bill Dannemeyer, an archconservative from Orange County, California, whose hostility toward gays thwarted the federal response to AIDS for many years. Dannemeyer was so obsessed, and so unpleasantly insistent, that Madigan and other moderate Republicans often let him have his way just so they wouldn't have to argue with him.

One tragedy of Dannemeyer's campaign was that AIDS is exactly the type of public health issue that should easily command bipartisan support. When Ed Madigan learned about it, in 1981, he immediately grasped the nature of the crisis. "We need to do something," he told me. "I can get Republicans to support legislation." When Dannemeyer weighed in, his determined priority was not research or prevention, but rather rounding up gay men and quarantining them on an island in the South Pacific, a proposal he called a press conference to announce. Dannemeyer was simply consumed by gay sex. In a speech titled, "What Homosexuals Do," he stood on the House floor and read graphic descriptions of sexual acts into the Congressional Record. At hearings, he constantly demanded to know, "When are we going to get names and force these people to register so that we have a list?"

In 1982, Republicans controlled the Senate. Ronald Reagan refused to so much as acknowledge the crisis, and would not even publicly utter the term "AIDS" until 1986. The only hope for government action lay in the House. But despite numerous hearings, it proved all but impossible to build support for legislation to fund research and prevention. Not all Republicans thought like Dannemeyer. But they always deferred to their leadership, and those leaders had no interest in confronting the crisis. One Republican committee member told me, "I'd like to help you, but I can't do anything on this issue because Dannemeyer will go after me."

Even more damaging than their effect on legislation was the quality of paranoid alarm that some Republicans imparted to the public sense of the AIDS disaster. Hearings designed to inform people about the emerging crisis wound up exacerbating many of the most harmful myths. Several news outlets reported that Dan Burton, an Indiana Republican, had stopped eating soup for fear that a waiter might give him AIDS, and he brought his own scissors to the House barber so that he would not acquire the disease from an earlier infected customer. Dannemeyer became convinced that AIDS was transmitted by spores and a carrier could pass it along simply by breathing on you. Although science suggested clearly that the virus was transmitted sexually or through the blood, he found the one doctor in the country sympathetic to his belief and had him testify, imbuing a crackpot view with credibility when the media reported on the hearing. More ominously, Dannemeyer wanted to criminalize the transmission of HIV.

Looked at in a larger context, this behavior was devastating. First, as health officials were racing to contain the outbreak and needed cooperation from the gay community, some Republicans were threatening arrest, internment, and registries that would force people out of the closet, jeopardizing their jobs, privacy, and health insurance. And second, at a time when many Americans feared the disease and longed for reliable information, their elected leaders fed the worst kind of hysteria by bringing scissors to the barbershop and hyperventilating about gay lifestyles.

The only AIDS bill that made its way into law in the early years was not formally an AIDS measure at all, but a piece of legislative legerdemain called the Public Health Emergency Trust Fund. The trust fund addressed a genuine problem: Because the federal budget runs in annual cycles that must be planned for well in advance, it is particularly ill suited to respond quickly to the outbreak of an epidemic. By lumping AIDS together with the Mount St. Helens explosion, Legionnaire's Disease, and Toxic Shock Syndrome, we successfully argued that situations often arise where public health agencies must respond to emergencies that cannot be budgeted for in advance. The initial appropriation for the new Public Health Emergency Trust Fund was a mere $30 million. But it worked as intended. In 1986, when AZT became the first drug approved to treat the AIDS virus, the trust bought emergency AZT for people who could not afford it.

FORTUNATELY, LEGISLATION IS NOT THE ONLY AVENUE A CONGRESS-man can pursue. My staff and I found other ways to address the crisis. One way we were able to direct more money to AIDS researchers was through the congressional budget process.

Thanks to our contacts in the agencies, we knew that many of the career people, and even the Reagan appointees who were public-health-minded, were stuck in an untenable situation. They were trying to get more money to study the epidemic, but Reagan's budget hawks would always intervene. Bound by their station, the health officials were obligated to defend whatever Reagan proposed, even when they knew it wasn't sufficient. When my staff visited the agencies, they'd tell us, "Here's what I believe but I'm not allowed to say."

Our imperative became finding a way to bring to light what they really believed. One way an administration controls information is by subjecting the testimony of government officials to political review beforehand. It may appear as though the Nobel laureate or the scientist from the CDC is saying precisely what he or she wants to say to the congressional committee, when in reality some twenty-four-year-old ideologue has censored and scrubbed his prepared testimony. The Reagan administration deployed many such minders. But anyone willing to go out to the agencies and get to know the people who worked there found it possible to have an honest back-and-forth. This is how we eventually hit upon a method for extracting honest testimony. We learned from a career official that questions relating to one's "professional judgment" were not subject to administration clearance. Thus arose an elaborate minuet. When I ventured onto sensitive terrain in hearings on the epidemic, I would preface each question with, "In your best professional judgment . . ." This magic phrase was so effective that we soon applied it across the board to Reagan appointees on every issue.

Another way that close ties to the agencies can pay off comes in the form of leaks. In 1985, a copy of the original budget request submitted by Department of Health and Human Services researchers studying AIDS was passed to my staff showing that it had been cut by two-thirds as it moved up the administration food chain. Reagan's top people were only asking for a fraction of what their scientists needed. Without showing my hand, I wrote to the secretary of health and human services asking her to explain how her agency had arrived at its paltry assessment for AIDS funding. Getting no reply, I announced plans to subpoena the budget documents and hold a hearing.

Among other things, the documents described how rapidly the epidemic was expanding. I hoped that the controversy we had drummed up over their release would draw national press attention to the issue. In the days leading up to the hearing, this did not appear to be the case. Jim Mason, an assistant secretary at Health and Human Services, had agreed to testify, knew that I had the budget documents, and probably had a good idea of my intention to rake him over the coals about the budget process. Unpleasant, yes, but what looked to be just another small battle in the larger fight over AIDS.

Then, days before the hearing, news broke that Rock Hudson was being treated for AIDS with experimental drugs in Paris (because no treatment for it was available in the United States). The ensuing uproar transformed the issue overnight. Suddenly, the whole world wanted to know about AIDS.

The shifting nature of the public's interest is an underappreciated force in public policy. It can drive a lawmaker to distraction. In the first meeting with Jim Curran in 1981 and in the field hearing afterward, we had heard alarming projections of just how the AIDS epidemic would unfold; by 1985 everything the experts had predicted would happen had come to pass. Not only West Hollywood but the entire country was now in the midst of a horrifying health crisis, but, because that crisis focused on gay men, news of it was constantly pushed aside. Rock Hudson changed that. By putting a famous face on the disease he did what we in Congress had thus far been unable to do, and seized the public's attention. Suddenly, you couldn't keep the cameras away. What was shaping up as a minor hearing with Mason instead received wall-to-wall coverage on the evening news.

While the publicity was invaluable from a public health standpoint, I was soon reminded how fickle such attention can be. Just after word leaked of Hudson's illness, a producer for one of the major Sunday news shows called to book me. "We want you on the show this Sunday if Rock Hudson turns out to have AIDS," she said. "But if it turns out he doesn't, then we won't need you."

UNEXPECTED DEVELOPMENTS LIKE THE DISCLOSURE OF ROCK Hudson's illness can have profound effects. Another such instance held even greater significance for the government's response to the crisis, although at the time I first encountered C. Everett Koop, I never imagined that Ronald Reagan's surgeon general would become one of the pivotal figures in the fight against AIDS.

The spring of 1981 was a period of crisis for Democrats. Beset by the Reagan Revolution and scrambling to limit the effects of the Stockman Black Book, we turned to the budget process. In my main area—health—Reagan's proposed cuts were as draconian as elsewhere. Democrats controlled the House and might have functioned as a braking mechanism. But on March 30, 1981, Reagan was shot by John Hinckley, Jr., and the outpouring of sympathy and support helped his budget to pass easily. We fell back on the reconciliation process.

Once the president's budget has passed and spending and revenue levels are established, the action shifts to Congress. The *size* of Reagan's cuts was now fixed, but the specifics of what programs would be cut and how they were funded was for Congress to determine. The budget and appropriations bill provided room to maneuver within those narrow confines.

The problem we faced was twofold: Reagan wanted to cut or eliminate numerous health programs, including (ironically, it seemed to me) a program that provided seed money to hospitals to set up trauma centers, which are extremely expensive; this program had helped fund the trauma center at George Washington University Hospital, which had saved Reagan's own life after he was shot. The other part of the problem was that Reagan wanted to change the way many federal programs were funded, shifting the mechanism from program-specific allotments (such as immunizations or TB control) to what are known as block grants—essentially, lump sum payments to the states.

Block grants are a perennial Republican favorite because they make federal programs politically much easier to cut. Let's say Congress provides $5 billion a year to the states for a child-hood nutrition program that Republicans don't like. That's a tough task, because the effect of so specific a cut is easy to dramatize: Kids go hungry. Now suppose the $5 billion is shifted into state block grants for nutrition. Absent a federal program stipulating how states spend the money, some will direct it to school lunch programs, others to obesity prevention, others to whatever programs they see fit. When the next budget cycle rolls around and Republicans want to halve that $5 billion, there is no longer a federal program to defend or a uniform effect that can be dramatized in a hearing or a television ad, because each state is now doing something different with its allotment. The debate becomes decontextualized, a fight over dollars and cents rather than hungry children—and that's a fight the Republicans always prefer.

In 1981, we fought back in several ways. To protect community health centers, for example, we performed a bit of political jujitsu by accepting the idea of block grant funding—only we attached such onerous provisions to the grants that no state would dream of applying for one, allowing the health centers to continue being funded as a discrete program.

Another approach was less subtle. When you can block an opponent's cherished bill or key appointee, a lot can be gained by simple horse trading. This is where C. Everett Koop came into play. Koop was Reagan's appointee for surgeon general. Though a doctor, he was a pediatric surgeon, not a public health specialist as is typical with surgeons general, and this unorthodox background, along with his outspoken opposition to abortion, made him a figure of great controversy. But Koop had a weakness: his age. Normally, Senate confirmation is all that's required for the post. But a provision in the law required that the surgeon general be younger than sixty-five, and Koop wasn't. To take office, he needed us to change the law. In exchange for this dispensation, I asked Koop to appear before the Health Subcommittee to answer questions about his views and qualifications. The Reagan administration refused to permit this.

As the weeks progressed and the reconciliation bill moved into conference, the pressure in Washington shifted from Democrats to Republicans, who needed the bill to pass in order to appear effective. Most people think of Congress as operating solely through the legislative process: Bills work their way through subcommittee, full committee, floor vote, a House-Senate conference, and, usually, a presidential signature to become law. But if all sides agree, a conference markup can be a vehicle for accomplishing all sorts of things that couldn't make it through the full legislative process. Republicans were eager to cut family planning programs that provide women with contraception, and the Senate bill already reflected that change. As the condition for including the Koop legislation, I insisted that these programs remain intact, not as block grants but as what are called federal "categorical" programs, which are harder to cut.

This bargain proved enormously beneficial for two reasons. The family planning programs survived intact. And Koop became an unexpected and heroic partner in the struggle against AIDS. Owing to the circumstances of our acquaintance, Koop and I did not initially like each other. But over time, I came to realize that I had misjudged him. When the epidemic hit, Koop, for all that he lacked in public health experience, instinctively grasped its dimensions. At a time when Reagan would not acknowledge the disease, Koop insisted that it would not restrict itself to the gay community, and shouldn't be ignored even if it did.

This was important because at that time conservatives viewed AIDS not as a public health issue but as an ideological one. They vigilantly guarded against anything they perceived as creating "special rights," or even basic conditions of equality, for gays. Koop was a stalwart witness at hearings and often the lone Republican dissenter from this view. The Republican line on AIDS throughout the 1980s was that it was a lifestyle issue for which its victims were to blame. Whenever Koop testified before Congress, conservatives tried to get him to repeat their sound bite that "AIDS is not a no-fault disease." "I think you're mistaken," he would reply. As Koop, a deeply religious man, would often say, "I'm the nation's doctor, not the nation's chaplain."

To his enduring credit, when Koop looked at AIDS he saw the same thing that epidemiologists like Jim Curran saw: the need to deal immediately and rationally with a real-time health crisis.

As the nation's doctor, the surgeon general has tremendous credibility and influence. Koop used his to fight AIDS, and later tobacco, speaking plainly and truthfully when Republicans were discouraged from doing so. It could not have been easy for him. By the end of his tenure, many conservatives despised him. Some Republicans in Congress even boycotted a dinner in his honor because he had done what the rest of the Reagan administration refused to do and confronted the AIDS problem. That is why Koop is today regarded as the model of what a surgeon general should be.

His example is also a reminder to politicians in both parties that it is important to have enough self-assurance and loyalty to basic principle to be able to change one's mind when the facts merit. I was wrong about Koop—and he turned out to make one of the most significant contributions in dealing with AIDS and the public's health.

THE STRUGGLE TO PASS MAJOR AIDS LEGISLATION WAS A LONG AND difficult one. During the 1980s, the Subcommittee on Health and the Environment held more than two dozen hearings on the disease, their subjects ranging from research needs to public health recommendations to how it would impact hospital emergency rooms and the insurance industry. At first we could do little more than use the chairman's power to hold oversight hearings to raise public awareness and gather expert testimony on how best to handle the crisis. Though often frustrating, this laid the groundwork for legislation to emerge. It's a good example of how oversight and legislation work in tandem to give force to such responsibilities as framing the government's response to AIDS.

By 1988, the thrust of what needed to be done was clear. In Washington, AIDS had become a palpable reality in ways not felt before; members of Congress from all over probably knew someone who was dying of it. But important progress was being made. Researchers had developed a reliable test for AIDS and a drug, AZT, to help treat it.

That year I introduced legislation designed to encourage more people to visit doctors and clinics for testing, counseling, and treatment. The focus on testing was not universally embraced—many in the gay community still harbored a deep distrust of government, thanks in large part to the ongoing efforts of people like Bill Dannemeyer who aimed to subject AIDS patients to federal registries, quarantine, and deportation. But epidemiologists believed that counseling and testing was the best approach from a public health standpoint, since it would allow people to protect themselves and their loved ones from spreading the disease. So that was the course we pursued.

At that time, the law offered little protection for someone with AIDS. There were no federal health privacy laws, no confidentiality standards, and nothing to prevent discrimination (the Americans with Disabilities Act would help rectify this, but not for two more years). People genuinely feared losing their jobs, housing, or custody of their children, so a confidentiality provision and a guarantee against discrimination were obvious additions to the bill. The idea was to bring people in by eliminating disincentives and then to pay for testing and counseling. Republicans balked. To a person, those on my subcommittee told me, "I'm with you on counseling, testing, and confidentiality, but I can't support you on a nondiscrimination clause because that would look like a 'gay rights' bill." So we reluctantly dropped nondiscrimination protections at the outset.

Though it lacked much Republican support, the bill made it through subcommittee and was narrowly approved by the full House. Ted Kennedy had sponsored an AIDS bill that cleared the Senate, but dealt only with funding for research. That spring the House and Senate bills went to conference, where I aimed to insert testing, counseling, and confidentiality into the final bill, and Republicans kept up their efforts to kill it. One morning during the markup, Dannemeyer arrived, arms bursting with videocassettes and comic books from the Gay Men's Health Crisis in New York City, apoplectic that these materials "erotized" safe sex—never mind that, lacking any federal funding, they did not fall under congressional purview. (Once, seated next to him at a hearing, I couldn't help myself and asked, "Bill, what are your thoughts on masturbation?" With a grave look, he turned to me and replied, "I don't think there's anything we can do about it.")

It was not Dannemeyer, however, but North Carolina senator Jesse Helms who brought down a comprehensive AIDS bill that year. Negotiations between the House and Senate teams had progressed to the point that an agreement looked imminent, when Helms placed a "hold" on the bill, preventing it from moving forward until all but the research provision had been stripped. "I don't want any confidentiality on these records," Helms declared. "Nothing at all." I was furious and let him know: "A lot of lives are going to be lost because of what you've done." He replied that they would be lost because of a "gay disease."

The following year, we began anew. AIDS had gained a morbid kind of momentum by now, to the point that metropolitan emergency rooms were being overwhelmed. As Koop and others had long predicted, AIDS did not limit itself to the gay community. Now it was straining the entire health system and clearly needed to be addressed.

As activists and interest groups came together to lobby for attention and support, the public perception of AIDS slowly began to shift. An important catalyst for this change was Ryan White, a thirteen-year-old boy from Kokomo, Indiana, who had acquired AIDS from a blood transfusion. White had been banned from public schools, whereupon he and his mother had responded by launching a public education campaign. An enormously compelling figure, Ryan White soon became the literal poster boy for the disease, changing many people's perception of AIDS because he so clearly did not fit the stereotype of the victim as a gay man or a drug user.

In 1989, we wrote a new bill that began with counseling, testing, confidentiality, and treatment, and later came to include research funding to study pediatric AIDS, since virtually none was available. On the Senate side, Kennedy introduced emergency impact assistance for hospitals. To gain Republican support, he approached Orrin Hatch of Utah. Lacking big cities, Utah hospitals were not yet being overrun, so they did not stand to receive emergency assistance. As a compromise with Hatch, Kennedy included block grants to the states so that even areas as yet unaffected by AIDS could also build an infrastructure to handle the epidemic when it arrived.

I, too, was concerned about getting Republicans on board.

Though bipartisanship seemed to fall into disfavor during the Bush years, my experience has always been that it is nearly impossible to pass major legislation without support from both parties. As I'd learned from watching my predecessor, Paul Rogers, getting everyone involved in a bill vastly improved the chance that it would become law.

This presented an obvious challenge: Bill Dannemeyer, the subcommittee's most vociferous member, wasn't about to cooperate on a bill, block grants or not. He continued to offer "grenade amendments" requiring mandatory AIDS testing. So we went above him, to the full committee level, and approached Norman Lent, a New York Republican who was ranking member of the House Energy and Commerce Committee, and whose district in Long Island was very much affected by AIDS. But it remained a tough sell to get a Republican's support for such legislation. One reason that Paul Rogers was so effective a chairman was his willingness—uncommon in Washington—to parcel out credit to other members. At around this time, an activist named Elizabeth Glaser approached my staff with a proposal regarding pediatric AIDS. I suggested that she take it to Lent, who could offer it as an amendment to our bill. A major impediment to Republican support was that AIDS still conjured images of drug users and gay men among many of their constituents. However, pediatric AIDS, as Lent understood, was a noncontroversial exception. By adding his amendment, we were able to build bipartisan support *around* Dannemeyer, further strengthening the bill.

Even then, its fate was unclear. Reagan was gone by now, but his successor, George H. W. Bush, did not support the legislation. And the Senate prospects once again looked iffy. The person who finally tipped the balance was a Republican senator from Indiana, Dan Coats. Coats had not planned to support the bill. But legend has it that Ted Kennedy persuaded him by offering to rename the legislation the Ryan White Comprehensive AIDS Resources Emergency (CARE) Act in honor of Coats's young constituent, a powerfully savvy ploy on two fronts. By the stroke of a pen, it shifted public attention from gay men and drug users to a thirteen-year-old boy who many already knew of and admired; renaming the bill after Ryan White also subtly pressured Coats to support it or risk looking callous in a way sure to be noticed back home. When Coats switched his vote, several others did, too—the support of so staunch a conservative as Coats provided political cover.

Ryan White died on April 8, 1990. Four months later, President Bush signed his act into law. The Ryan White CARE Act was initially adopted for a five-year period, and has since been reauthorized three times. It continues to provide assistance to hundreds of thousands of low-income and uninsured people living with HIV and AIDS and, as the profile of the disease has shifted, spreading into rural areas, it has been updated to keep pace.

CHAPTER 4

The Orphan Drug Act

 ONE FALL MORNING IN 1979, BILL CORR, A MEMBER OF MY subcommittee staff, was sitting at his desk when the phone rang. A panicked caller named Muriel Seligman told him that her son Adam suffered from a rare neurological disorder known as Tourette's syndrome, for which no treatment was available in the United States. Adam's doctor had told them that a drug called Pimozide, sold in Canada, helped alleviate the involuntary motor tics, cursing, and guttural noises that are symptoms of Tourette's. So Muriel Seligman, feeling she had no alternative, had asked a friend to fly to Canada to obtain Pimozide for her son. She was frantic because earlier that day customs agents at San Francisco International Airport had intercepted the friend as he returned and seized the medication because it was not approved for use in the United States. As a constituent, she was calling to demand my help. "They took the drug that my son needs," she said. "What are you going to do about it?"

A frequent complaint about Congress is that it does not respond to people's needs. But Mrs. Seligman's phone call demonstrates that this is not always the case. The concern for her son that prompted a call to her congressman set in motion a chain of events that culminated in legislation that addressed not only Adam's plight but those of millions of other Americans just like him who were silently suffering from rare diseases.

Disturbed by the Seligmans' story, my staff began by looking into the obvious question: If Canada offered a safe and effective treatment for Tourette's syndrome, why wasn't one available in the United States? The answer soon became clear. Tourette's was an ailment that afflicted so few people that it did not hold sufficient profit potential to entice any U.S. pharmaceutical company into the costly process of developing and gaining approval for a treatment. Tourette's fell into the broad category of "orphan diseases" whose victims had little hope of ever finding a treatment or cure because their numbers were so few. The situation was especially tragic, we learned, because scientists who discovered promising new treatments for orphan diseases often could not interest profit-minded drugmakers. These products thus became known as "orphan drugs," and pharmaceutical companies rarely pursued them, even in cases when a foreign drug like Pimozide demonstrated clear potential.

When a member of Congress confronts this sort of dilemma, the first challenge is to gain a sufficient understanding of the problem, and then to figure out what the government can do about it. In an effort to learn more about orphan diseases and how we might help those stricken by them, the Health and the Environment Subcommittee scheduled a preliminary hearing on Capitol Hill in June 1980. We invited Adam Seligman, and several doctors, government officials, and representatives of the few organized rare-disease groups we could find to testify.

What we learned at the hearing was that although the federal government and the private pharmaceutical industry spent hundreds of millions of dollars a year for biomedical research and drug development, our country's system of discovering and developing new drugs contained an important flaw: It did not account for the inherent financial disincentives to producing orphan drugs, and therefore failed to serve millions of people like Adam Seligman who suffered from rare diseases. Since no government policy addressed this shortcoming, creating a mechanism to facilitate the development of these drugs seemed a promising line of pursuit.

Every day that Congress is in session, members are constantly being barraged by problems like this one that demand their urgent attention. The number of these competing claims unfortunately far outstrips the time and resources that Congress can apply to them. One benefit of a hearing like the first one we held on the orphan drug problem is that it can take an abstract policy issue like pharmaceutical development and bring it vividly to life with searing human examples of who it affects and why Congress must act on it.

When his turn came to testify, Adam Seligman took a seat before the members of the subcommittee. At eighteen years old, Adam was slender, dark-haired, and handsome, but the simple act of carrying on a conversation required enormous energy; he was constantly fighting through the frequent outbursts and loud guttural noises that Tourette's inflicts, which made his willingness to testify before Congress all the more courageous.

I began by asking Adam to describe what his life had been like. He recounted the story in stages. At age eight, the first signs that something was not right. The tics that began soon after, developed into muscle spasms, and finally into the horrific "dystonic reactions"—the doctor's term for the sudden jerks that snapped his neck back so violently that he couldn't breathe. The emergency room visits that ensued, and the procession of mystified doctors who could not even give his mother a name for her son's affliction. The years of hopelessness and fear continued until, at age fourteen, the genetic clues finally yielded a diagnosis. His eighty-two-year-old grandfather had been the unlocking key. Long ago, doctors had told the old man that the tremors in his hands and feet were caused by Saint Vitus' Dance. But Adam's new specialist recognized Tourette's. Haldol had eased the tremors, but brought fatigue, depression, blurred vision—made it impossible to function. Adam had had to repeat senior year. Pimozide was a magic elixir. He tore through two years of high school in nine months and, just before the hearing, graduated with extra credit. But the Pimozide was gone now, and the symptoms returning.

"What will you do without Pimozide?" I asked him.

"I don't know," he replied. "When the tics start to get really bad again I will have to go back on Haldol, which I would really not like to do."

Amid the sadness of cases like Adam's were also tales of great heroism and perseverance on behalf of the ill, such as that of Dr. Melvin Van Woert. Like Adam Seligman, Dr. Van Woert's patient suffered from a rare but treatable condition, in this case a neurological disorder called myoclonus, so debilitating that it had forced her into a wheelchair. Though a treatment existed, no pharmaceutical company considered it commercially viable, and so none would agree to bring it to market. For years, Dr. Van Woert, relying on grants from private foundations, had hand-mixed the drug himself with ingredients purchased from a biochemical supply house that ordinarily serviced veterinarians, and had kept his patient out of her wheelchair.

The day's testimony convinced most of us that this was a clear case of a problem that Congress could play a constructive role in solving. Next we needed to figure out the best course of action. Only then could we turn to the greatest challenge of all: figuring out how to build public momentum to fix a medical issue that even many doctors were not aware of.

*   *   *

THAT FIRST HEARING, IN JUNE 1980, DREW A SPARSE CROWD AND little public notice. Only the *Los Angeles Times* sent a reporter, and only because Adam Seligman was a local resident. But this was enough to deliver an unexpected boost. The next day, a Hollywood writer and producer named Maurice Klugman happened upon the *Times* article and was moved by what he read. Klugman himself was battling a rare form of cancer. A producer of the hit television drama *Quincy M.E.,* which starred his brother, the actor Jack Klugman, as a crusading medical examiner, he decided to write an episode of the show devoted to Tourette's syndrome and the orphan disease problem. At the end of the episode, a message explained to viewers that the story was based on real events and invited them to write in if they wanted to help. In the weeks and months after the show aired, thousands of letters poured into the *Quincy* production studio from viewers eager to help raise public awareness.

In the meantime, I used my chairmanship of the Health and the Environment Subcommittee to press ahead. I was not the only member of Congress concerned about orphan diseases. Elizabeth Holtzman, a Democrat from New York, had previously introduced a bill calling for the government to develop orphan drugs through the National Institutes of Health. Holtzman's rationale was that NIH scientists already conducted biochemical research using drugs; she wanted to expand the agency's responsibilities to include developing them for the market as well. Holtzman retired in 1980, but appealed to a colleague, Ted Weiss, a Manhattan Democrat, to reintroduce her bill after she left. Weiss had done so, but the measure had not gotten far because Congress was reluctant to provide the considerable outlay that a major new government initiative would require and because some members wondered whether the private sector might not do a better job. The fundamental question that we needed to decide in order to put together effective legislation was whether government or the pharmaceutical industry was better suited to the task of developing orphan drugs.

To learn more about the Holtzman-Weiss approach and the private industry alternative, I organized a second hearing for the spring of 1981. Orphan drugs remained an obscure issue, so we needed to draw more attention to the problem to foster a sense of urgency and pressure Congress to act. The *Quincy* episode devoted to Tourette's syndrome was scheduled to run on March 4, 1981. So we decided to hold the hearing the following week and invited Quincy himself—Jack Klugman—to testify, along with pharmaceutical industry representatives, government officials, and a broad group of people with orphan diseases.

Hollywood celebrities are so prevalent on Capitol Hill these days that they rarely cause much of a stir. But in 1981, the appearance of a bona fide television star like Jack Klugman at a congressional hearing was a major news event. On the appointed day, *The New York Times* ran a front-page story on Klugman and the orphan disease problem. While our first hearing, nine months earlier, had taken place before a nearly empty room, this time we arrived to find it jam-packed with cameras and reporters.

This was, of course, precisely the effect we had intended by inviting Klugman to appear. Orphan diseases had been ignored or overlooked for years. Now, suddenly, they were in the spotlight. Klugman's testimony had a mesmerizing effect, and not just on the news media—in a rare moment of levity, my colleague Jim Scheuer of New York began asking the star witness scientific questions, as if he were a real medical examiner, rather than an actor who portrayed one on television.

But even Klugman's star wattage could not overshadow

the testimony of those stricken by orphan diseases, who spoke next. After Adam Seligman appeared before Congress the previous summer, the news had spread to people with all sorts of rare ailments that a few people in Washington had at last noticed their predicament and wanted to help. The first hearing had featured testimony from just one other victim besides Adam because we had had difficulty finding others; no national group existed then to organize and advocate on behalf of this underserved population. This time, however, the hearing room was filled with victims, many of them children, of some of the rarest and least understood disorders known to medicine—people with terrible skin ailments, crippling cancers, elephantiasis, and conditions that caused webbed fingers and internal organs. They had in common the exotic nature of their maladies.

At the time, Tourette's afflicted only about 100,000 people, not nearly enough to interest drug companies, but still more than many of the other diseases and conditions that were represented that day by victims and their families. They included muscular dystrophy, a congenital disorder that weakens the muscles; cystic fibrosis, a deadly hereditary disorder (40,000); spina bifida, a congenital neurological condition (27,500); Huntington's chorea, a degenerative disease of the mind and nervous system (14,000); ALS, better known as Lou Gehrig's disease (9,000). Then there were the truly obscure ailments. Prader-Willi syndrome, a fatal ailment that causes huge weight gain in children, afflicted about 2,000 a year; Wilson's disease, an abnormal accumulation of copper in the liver and brain, just 1,000; and cystinosis, a genetic disorder that usually causes kidney failure by age ten, struck about 100 children a year.

One by one, victims of these diseases and their family members described lives of helpless isolation, driven by the unending and often futile search for answers about their condition and medical care to treat it. Most had nowhere to turn. The sights, sounds, and personal stories brought many of us to the point of tears. It was as if someone had pulled back a curtain to reveal an entire segment of society that no one knew was there: Gathered together in a congressional hearing room before the national media were human beings with diseases so disabling or disfiguring that they never came out in public. In my thirty-five years as a congressman, I have never witnessed a more powerful scene.

AT THE SAME TIME THAT WE WERE USING THE HEARING PROCESS to conduct a public inquiry and raise awareness, Bill Corr and others on my subcommittee staff embarked on a major survey of drug companies, federal research agencies, and university scientists to gain a thoroughgoing understanding of how the drug development process worked and why it was not yielding treatments for rare diseases. We wanted to know how many orphan drugs existed, why promising compounds often languished in the laboratory, and which entity—government or industry—was ultimately better equipped to address the problem.

From the outset, we met stiff resistance. Drug company executives didn't want to appear before Congress for fear of looking mean-spirited. Instead, representatives of the industry's trade group, the Pharmaceutical Manufacturers Association (PMA), claimed that, contrary to all outward appearances, drug companies in fact had no problem at all developing treatments for orphan diseases, and would oppose any legislation aimed at making them do more. This is an unfortunate and all too common refrain from trade groups in any industry and a big reason why such organizations often pose the greatest obstacle to good legislation. Because trade groups exist to represent the interests of an entire industry, their main concern is maintaining the happiness of all their members. Even legislation that is supported by a broad array of drug companies, and opposed by only a vocal few, will typically engender opposition from the PMA: Trade groups always push to weaken a bill to the point where none of their members object to it, which is why they are often such a negative force in the legislative process.

Our survey nevertheless laid out the full extent of the problem. Doctors had identified about two thousand rare diseases. We turned up 134 drugs used to treat them, forty-seven of which were approved for use in the United States. Contrary to industry claims, only ten of these forty-seven drugs had been developed and marketed by U.S. pharmaceutical companies in the last decade. Here was clear proof that the current system wasn't working.

The survey also revealed other important reasons why drugmakers did not develop most of the promising orphan compounds that scientists discovered. In addition to serving markets too small to make desirable targets, we found out that many orphan drugs were not patentable or that their patents had expired, and thus offered much smaller profit potential. By law, most drug patents provided the manufacturer an extremely valuable seventeen-year period of exclusive control. The clock started ticking when the patent was awarded. But since orphan drug development was seldom cost-effective and therefore not a priority, patented compounds that might have yielded treatments for orphan diseases often lingered undeveloped until the seventeen-year window had closed. Lacking the potential to produce a temporary windfall, developing the orphan drug became an even harder sell.

Finally, we learned that drugmakers had an understandably difficult time meeting FDA testing requirements. It's impossible to run hundreds or thousands of patient tests on a drug designed to treat a disease that only affects a few dozen people each year. Consequently, the clinical trials surrounding orphan drugs were often fraught with great uncertainty. The risk that the FDA might not accept the improvised testing that orphan drug development sometimes entailed had an additional chilling effect on pharmaceutical companies.

One purpose of the survey was to shed some light on the question of whether government or industry was better equipped to develop treatments for rare diseases. Holtzman and Weiss had shown that a compelling argument could be made for having the NIH do the job. But our investigation convinced us that this was not the best approach because NIH, as a research institute, had no experience in developing drugs for the commercial market. The true expertise and resources lay in the private sector, so finding a way to interest pharmaceutical companies in pursuing treatments seemed to offer the best chance of success. We wrote the Orphan Drug Act with this in mind, creating a host of new incentives for private industry, and introduced our bill in December 1981.

The secret to crafting legislation that works is not ramming through a partisan bill, but rather designing one that is acceptable to all parties. The pharmaceutical industry had made clear that it did not want a new law. But we intended to pass one anyway. From the outset, our challenge was clear: We had to find a way to persuade private drugmakers, which actively opposed our efforts, to address orphan drugs, and believed that the key to changing their outlook was to design legislation that accounted for the financial and procedural hurdles they faced.

The easy way to gain industry support would have been to lower the FDA approval standards for orphan drugs. Many patient groups, desperate for a cure, would have accepted this as the only feasible way to bring these drugs to market. But weaker safety and effectiveness standards would have further imperiled sick people's health and tempted drugmakers to abuse the loophole, so while flexibility is the key to any deal, we vowed that safety and efficacy was the one area where we would brook no compromise. Shortcuts were out of the question.

Instead, our bill encompassed three major incentives for pharmaceutical companies, each addressing a specific impediment to orphan drug development that we had uncovered in our survey and hearings. The first component eliminated the patent problem by providing a "market exclusivity provision" guaranteeing the drug's manufacturer a seven-year monopoly— in addition the clock would not start ticking until much later in the regulatory process, after the drug had received FDA approval. The second component eased the regulatory burden by encouraging pharmaceutical companies to consult with the FDA during the clinical testing phase, collaborating on the tricky question of how best to run tests when a disease affects only a small population and thereby removing the element of uncertainty. This was an admittedly unusual approach, since the FDA is a regulatory body charged with rendering impartial judgment—it was a bit like collaborating with the teacher who was about to grade your test. But we thought it was the best way to remove the deterrent. Toward that end, the third component of the bill was a 90 percent tax credit designed to pay most of the cost of clinical trials. To encourage research and innovation, the bill also established an Office of Rare Diseases at NIH.

THE KLUGMAN HEARING HAD A GALVANIZING EFFECT THAT INstantly improved the bill's prospects. No longer were orphan diseases the obscure problem they had been just a year earlier. A third hearing, held in March 1982 to highlight our survey findings, improved them further, since our proposed solution did not entail an expensive new government program and offered a package of financial incentives and cost reductions that the Pharmaceutical Manufacturers Association, after some discussion, decided was acceptable after all. Ordinarily, a bill would start out in subcommittee, work its way through full committee, and eventually come to the House floor. But the subcommittee and full committee chairmen can, if they so desire, jointly agree to speed up the process by taking up a bill directly in committee, which is what happened to the orphan drug bill. On September 15, John Dingell, the chairman of the House Energy and Commerce Committee, called up the bill. Seeing widespread support, Dingell called for a voice vote, which is the easiest way to move ahead when you have overwhelming consensus and nobody in the opposition demands to have the vote recorded. As it turned out, no opposition materialized, and the measure passed unanimously.

Nevertheless, popular bills can still run into unexpected trouble or delay. Outside factors like news events can suddenly alter the political landscape and derail legislation that once seemed certain to land on the president's desk. Even in ordinary circumstances a bill's author loses a measure of control when legislation is reported out of committee. The next step on the procedural path is the Rules Committee, which determines the amount of time allotted for floor debate, the number of amendments that can be offered, and sometimes even the specific nature of those amendments. Rules votes are invariably party-line affairs, so the tyranny of the majority always threatens to intrude.

One way to avoid all this is to ask the speaker to place the bill on the suspension calendar, a fast-tracking process for legislation that has at least two-thirds support of the House. The suspension calendar literally "suspends" the rules, forbidding any amendments, limiting debate over a bill to forty minutes (twenty for each side) and bringing the measure to a prompt vote. The Orphan Drug Act of 1982, as our bill was now officially titled, was placed on the suspension calendar and approved on September 28, 1982.

To become law, an identical bill must pass both houses of Congress. Normally, a senator and a congressman introduce similar bills whose differences are reconciled in a House-Senate conference if both chambers approve them. The compromise bill that emerges from conference then must pass each chamber before it can obtain a presidential signature. Sometimes the back-and-forth between the House and Senate gets tricky.

Since no senator had introduced orphan drug legislation, our House bill was sent over to the Senate for consideration, whereupon it was held at the Senate desk, pending the decision of the Senate's majority party. A senator can request that a bill held at the desk be assigned to the relevant committee for action. If no such request is made, the bill stays at the desk until the majority leader calls it up for a vote. Since Republicans controlled the Senate, the bill's fate lay in the hands of Orrin Hatch of Utah, chairman of the Senate Labor and Human Resources Committee, which had jurisdiction over drug legislation.

Hatch signaled his interest in the orphan drug measure—a potentially worrisome development because we needed his support. We were relieved to learn, however, that rather than block the bill, Hatch intended to use it as a vehicle for a series of unrelated initiatives that he and an assortment of colleagues wanted to pass. This is a common legislative tactic when a non-controversial bill has passed one chamber and awaits action in the other, and Hatch used it more frequently than most. But his benign intentions did not yet get us out of the woods. Any changes to the bill, even ones that were not intended to kill it, could nonetheless have unintended consequences that would bring about the same result.

Hatch's main interest turned out to be an amendment establishing a cancer research and screening program for 200,000 people in and around Utah who were exposed to radiation from nuclear weapons testing in the 1950s, and, in many cases, later developed cancer. Once again, this came as a relief. The program struck me as an eminently worthy idea. But the next amendment stopped us cold. Bob Dole and Russell Long, respectively the chairman and ranking member of the Senate Finance Committee, had prevailed upon Hatch to strike the 90 percent tax credit we had included for clinical trials of orphan drugs—a move intended to protect their bureaucratic turf, since tax policy ordinarily falls under the purview of the Finance Committee, through which the bill had not passed. We considered the tax credit to be the central feature of our bill, the mechanism by which government could finally persuade pharmaceutical makers to develop orphan drugs. In lieu of a tax credit, the Dole-Long amendment authorized a $50 million grant program, which, to the uninitiated, might seem a meaningless distinction. But Dole and Long understood the crucial difference: A tax credit can simply be written into law and take effect immediately, whereas a grant requires not only an authorization but an appropriation as well—that is, Congress not only had to authorize the money, but hand it over, too, which would entail a whole new legislative battle. Dole and Long knew that, on its own, a $50 million authorization wasn't good for much, and by swapping it for the tax credit, they would effectively neuter the bill. The Senate's unanimous approval of the Hatch-modified bill on October 1 made that fear a reality.

This meant that to have any chance of saving the bill, we would have to restore the tax credits and then send the updated measure back to the Senate for approval. Adding to the pressure was the impending *adjournment sine die*, the Latin term used in Congress to mean the end of a two-year session. If we could not repair and repass the orphan drug bill by year's end, the session would expire and we would have to start from the beginning in the next Congress. So began the real negotiations that settled the Orphan Drug Act.

The narrow time frame confronting us necessitated joint House-Senate negotiations. Because so many committees now held a stake in the bill, my House colleagues and I had to contend with representatives from the Senate Finance, Ways and Means, and Labor and Human Resources committees—with Hatch still controlling the bill's fate in the Senate; and the House Ways and Means Committee, which oversees most tax issues. Through most of October, our efforts to restore the tax credit didn't get very far. Meanwhile, the calendar provided a grim daily reminder that time was running out.

There isn't much that a House member can do to force a senator to act on a bill. But Jack Klugman hit upon a novel idea. He and his brother wrote a second episode of *Quincy*, which aired on October 27 and once again reflected events in Congress. This time the story line revolved around an orphan drug bill that was being held up by a heartless senator. In the show's pivotal scene, the senator dismisses the need for orphan drugs, telling Klugman, "Nobody cares about this bill." A righteous Klugman fires back, "Look outside." Peering down from his office window, the senator sees a large crowd chanting and holding signs that read, "We Want the Orphan Drug Act." To shoot the scene, the show's producers hired five hundred people who really did suffer from rare diseases to serve as extras.

Arriving in the middle of these tense negotiations, the *Quincy* episode brought a new wave of public pressure for Congress to act. In the wake of the show, the talks picked up again, and a deal gradually emerged: The cost of clinical trials for orphan drugs would be subsidized by a 50 percent tax credit, a 50 percent tax deduction, and a much smaller $12 million grant program—the reduced tax credit and grant program face-saving measures for our opponents, who agreed to a very good deal for our side. On December 14, the updated bill passed the House; two days later—and this time, without any changes—it passed the Senate, too. As *sine die* arrived and members returned home for the holidays, what was now officially the Waxman-Hatch Orphan Drug Act moved on to the president.

EVEN AS THE HOUSE-SENATE NEGOTIATIONS GAINED MOMENTUM, ominous signs were emanating from the White House. In late fall, Richard Schweiker, Reagan's secretary of health and human services, had called with a warning. "I want this bill, I think it's great," Schweiker told me. "But I've been told by the president to prepare the veto message."

In an unfortunate irony, the White House opposition had nothing to do with the orphan drug component, but rather stemmed from Hatch's cancer testing and screening program for those whose health had suffered from nuclear weapons testing. Reagan feared the program would leave the government culpable for thousands of cancer patients and exact an enormous toll on the federal budget. But since no president could utter anything so heartless in public, the White House claimed to object to the tax credits, whose cost the Congressional Budget Office had estimated at $15 million. Strange as it seemed to many of us, Reagan's public stance had him willing to ignore the health needs of hundreds of thousands of sick people in order to save the budgetary equivalent of a drop in the ocean. Regardless, organizing an effort to change his mind became our immediate imperative.

Lobbying a president on legislation is not all that different than lobbying congressional colleagues, except that the president is much harder to reach. The goal is still to apply pressure in any way that you can. For this task, our Senate partner, Orrin

Hatch, now became an invaluable ally. Along with being a Republican, Hatch was a forceful advocate who threw himself into the effort to persuade the White House.

The public nature of our campaign for orphan drugs also helped to lend pressure. One useful side effect of the action in Congress was that it led 140 rare-disease groups to band together as the National Organization for Rare Disorders. NORD took out full-page ads in major newspapers, including in California, where Reagan was spending the holidays, urging the president not to be "the Grinch who stole Christmas" by vetoing the bill.

I, too, tried to persuade the president, publicly and privately. To draw maximum attention, Jack Klugman, Adam Seligman, and I held a Christmas Eve press conference in Los Angeles where I delivered remarks designed to cast the issue against the backdrop of the holiday season: "Last week, years of effort to help people with rare diseases culminated with the unanimous passage by both houses of Congress of the Orphan Drug Act. I had hoped for this Los Angeles press conference to be a joyful celebration of the victory for which all the groups represented here today worked very hard. Unfortunately, it is my duty to tell you that the battle may not yet be over. I have been unable to obtain any reassurance from the White House that the president will sign this bill. Incredible as it may seem, there are reliable reports that even as we prepare to mark the Christmas holidays, the White House is preparing to kill this humanitarian legislation. . . . We need to write, call, and send telegrams to the White House. We also need to urge television stations, key news-oriented radio stations, and the press to give full coverage to this vital issue."

Often, the most effective leverage in a situation such as this does not come from political opponents, but from supporters, especially those who have personal relationships with the president. Every New Year's Eve, the Reagans attended a party thrown by the Annenberg family in Palm Springs. A Republican businessman from my district named Ted Cummings was part of that crowd, so I called him and said, "I'd like you to talk to President Reagan at the New Year's Eve party." Cummings protested that all talk of politics would be strictly off limits at the party. Don't worry, I assured him, this wasn't politics but a situation where people suffering from rare diseases had a chance to get lifesaving medication. Cummings thought it over, but wouldn't commit. "We just don't do that kind of thing," he said.

I never found out what transpired at the Annenbergs' party. Some things are better left as mysteries. But just after New Year's, Schweiker got a call from the White House telling him to prepare a new message: The president would sign the bill; and on January 4, 1983, the Orphan Drug Act became law.

AS SEVERAL PEOPLE REMARKED AT THE TIME, THE DRAMATIC RES-cue effort had all the hallmarks of a Hollywood ending. Afterward, Jack Klugman and everyone else who played a role in passing the legislation gathered for a huge party.

But the real Hollywood ending unfolded over the next twenty-five years, as the Orphan Drug Act took effect and produced enormous benefits. Some were anticipated. Since 1983, the FDA has approved more than three hundred orphan drugs—up from ten the decade prior—with 1,100 more currently under development. Rare-disease work at NIH has expanded significantly due to the increased visibility and funding. In January 1985, Pimozide became one of the first orphan drugs to gain FDA approval under the new law, and continues to be widely prescribed as a treatment for Tourette's syndrome. Another group that saw early benefit from the law was the growing number of those with AIDS. One of the first drugs approved to treat the disease, AZT, was developed and marketed as an orphan drug.

The Orphan Drug Act has worked so well that it has served as a model for similar programs in the European Union, Japan, and Australia. Under the leadership of Abbey Meyers, an early activist for Tourette's who was instrumental in helping us pass the law, the National Organization for Rare Disorders has gone on to achieve global renown, and now organizes the latest drug research from all over the world.

Nearly as significant have been the law's unexpected benefits. The pharmaceutical industry, for instance, has come full circle and now lauds the Orphan Drug Act. While our aim had been to encourage the big drugmakers to develop promising compounds, only about 15 percent of the applications for orphan drugs today derive from the major pharmaceutical companies. Instead, many smaller firms have come into being specifically to develop them.

One reason for this, likewise unexpected, is the degree to which the law's exclusivity provision has fostered new drugs. The critical legislative battle was fought over tax credits for clinical trials because we believed that this expense posed the single greatest impediment to developing orphan compounds. As it turned out, however, drug prices began rising steadily in the early 1980s, generating bigger and bigger profits for pharmaceutical companies the higher they climbed. Consequently, many drugs that were once considered financially unviable suddenly held new profit potential, and the need to subsidize clinical trials diminished.

Instead, the law's guarantee of seven years' market exclusivity became the key issue for its success. In 1985 the Orphan Drug Act was amended to include biological as well as chemical drugs, which helped give rise to an entire new industry, biotechnology drugs. In the 1980s, as biotech products began to emerge, there was uncertainty about how patent laws would apply to them. While today's patent protection for biotech drugs are robust, at the time they were perceived to be so unpredictable that many companies, especially small upstarts, had little confidence in the market protections available to them. The Orphan Drug Act's guarantee of seven years' protection from competition functioned as an effective substitute, sheltering smaller firms as they developed drugs for orphan diseases that often became profitable. (Many orphan diseases lend themselves to biotech treatments.) Some of the most successful biotech drugs, such as synthetic human growth hormone, came into being as orphan drugs.

Even successful legislation needs periodic updating to close loopholes, address unanticipated shortcomings, and keep up with changing circumstances. This can be a major battle in its own right. The protections outlined in the Orphan Drug Act were designed to make drug development economically feasible where otherwise it might not have been. Some manufacturers took advantage of the protections to inflate profits and stave off competition, reaping windfalls far in excess of development costs that consumers and the federal government (through Medicare and Medicaid) end up subsidizing in the form of higher prices. Another dishonest tactic was to claim orphan drug status for a narrowly defined treatment group and then pile up additional orphan designations for different applications of the same drug, a technique known as "salami slicing."

In 1990, we introduced a package of amendments that would have created "shared exclusivity," allowing firms to develop drugs simultaneously and lower prices through competition. We also tried to give the FDA power to reassess orphan drug exclusivity after three years to determine whether market protection was still necessary. This would have ensured that the law functioned as intended, helping to create drugs for small rare-disease populations and limiting opportunities to exploit it. The House and Senate passed the bill unanimously. But President George H. W. Bush vetoed it after heavy lobbying from the pharmaceutical industry. The episode serves as a stark reminder of the industry's tremendous power, and why it is important, when crafting legislation, never to give too much away. In all my years as a legislator, I can't recall a single example of a law where, when drug companies were granted excessive government concessions, we ever managed to scale them back later.

The Orphan Drug Act nevertheless remains an example of government at its finest, demonstrating how Congress applies itself to solve overlooked, but deeply important, problems that affect millions of Americans. Muriel Seligman's phone call became the catalyst for new a law that, twenty-five years later, has helped transform not only the lives of families like the Seligmans, but the entire way in which the drug industry approaches the development of new medications for orphan diseases.

CHAPTER 5

The Clean Air Act

NOTHING IS MORE FUNDAMENTAL THAN THE AIR WE breathe, the food we eat, and the water we drink—but until 1970, nothing limited the amount of pollution that could be released into the air. The Clean Air Act of 1970 stands as landmark legislation because it established the first system to regulate pollution from industrial plants and cars. In 1977, Paul Rogers, my old subcommittee chairman, took a lead in strengthening the law by cutting down on vehicle tailpipe emissions. As a native of Los Angeles, I was pleased to have played a small part, and recalled the days when Uncle Al had faced off with local industry. By the time I entered Congress, both parties recognized the importance of clean air.

Ronald Reagan did not. During his presidential campaign, Reagan betrayed his lack of regard for the environment by claiming that trees cause pollution. Soon after sweeping into office on an anti-government wave, he led a serious assault on the Clean Air Act. Reagan wanted to attack the philosophical core of the law—the idea that its central purpose was to protect people's health—and replace it with a cost-based standard more amenable to business. He wanted to double the amount of pollution cars could emit; double the pollution permitted in national parks; and relax controls on nearly every source of industrial emissions. Most frightening to anyone who cared about the environment was the near certainty that he could do it. American industry eagerly lined up behind him. Republicans had gained expanded numbers in Congress after routing Democrats in the election. And a powerful Democrat, John Dingell of Michigan, champion of the auto industry and chairman of the House Energy and Commerce Committee, had agreed to sponsor Reagan's bill. Advocates of clean air knew no darker time than the early days of 1981.

Yet the rollback never materialized. Reagan's assault was turned against him, and energized a decade-long battle that culminated in the toughest environmental law in American history. The Clean Air Act Amendments of 1990 reversed the causes of acid rain, ozone depletion, and smog, while imposing further significant restrictions on pollution from cars and trucks. By the mid-1990s it was clear that this was not just America's toughest environmental legislation, but also its most effective: Dramatic reductions in pollution came at a fraction of the cost that industry and experts had predicted.

The story of the Clean Air Act is one of the best illustrations of how Congress really works—how the oversight and legislative processes can combine to solve immense societal problems; how industry and its allies in Congress attack the regulatory system, and how they can be stopped; and how major acts of legislation, though they may take years to push through, provide benefits that last for generations. From my own perspective, the fight to renew the Clean Air Act is also an adventure tale, complete with several near-death experiences, years of careful plotting and brinkmanship, and the eventual triumph of David over Goliath. Above all, the story serves as a reminder that no matter how gloomy the outlook or fearsome the opposition of the White House, powerful members of Congress, or the private sector, landmark legislation can be attained through organization, skill, and hard work.

THE GREATEST MISCONCEPTION ABOUT MAKING LAWS IS THE ASsumption that most problems have clear solutions, and reaching compromise mainly entails splitting the difference between partisan extremes. This is rarely the case, and legislation crafted this way usually fails. "Meeting in the middle" doesn't work for the simple reason that it invariably neglects to solve whatever problem raised the issue in the first place. Take the problem of smog. If 200 million tons of pollution must be climinated to clean the air, and industry wants to emit 100 million more, any splitting of the difference would effectively make things worse: The offending industry would wind up being saddled with additional costs, and the air wouldn't be noticeably cleaner. Nobody wins. Successful legislation, on the other hand, would find a way to solve the problem and clean the air without putting anyone out of business or costing anyone a job. This was the challenge that lay ahead of us in 1981. But first we had to stop Reagan.

What made the new president's coalition so imposing was its broad support in Congress. Important leaders in both parties had committed to undoing the 1970 law. From outside, legislative clashes are usually assumed to take place between the two parties; but the reality is that regional loyalties, not partisan ones, often draw the congressional battle lines. Such was the case with clean air. John Dingell, a Democrat, sided with Ronald Reagan, a Republican, because he represented the auto industry, and in 1981 the major automakers were reeling from a severe recession. Chrysler had teetered on the brink of bankruptcy, while Ford and GM were laying off thousands of workers. To Dingell and other Rust Belt Democrats, the conservative push to weaken environmental regulations presented an opportunity for them to ease the economic burden on some important constituents.

As chairman of the Energy and Commerce Committee, environmental legislation came under Dingell's purview. So in addition to the automotive industry, he was the point man for the oil, coal, steel, power, and chemical industries as well. Initially, this was a source of strength. Industry presented a unified front because Reagan had promised something for each interest. But privately, each worried that its interest would be sacrificed if the bill ran into trouble. It became one of our primary tactics to exploit this fear.

Regional differences helped our side, too, though we lacked anything like the nationwide momentum of the Reagan Revolution. Jerry Lewis, a Republican from Southern California also under the shadow of Los Angeles smog, agreed to co-sponsor a competing bill with me. And one of few reassuring moments early on came in conversation with Robert Stafford, a Vermont Republican whom the new Republican majority had made chair of the Senate's Environment and Public Works Committee. Stafford pledged to do whatever he could to block the Dingell bill that both of us feared would emerge from the House.

WHEN CONFRONTED BY A STEAMROLLER, AS WE WERE ABOUT TO be, you first need to slow its momentum. There are two ways to go about this. One way is to stall, by whipping up a blizzard of amendments that demand the committee's attention, while pursuing every parliamentary maneuver in the rule book to delay the proceedings. The other way is to win a skirmish, to prevail on an amendment and force the other side to have to fall back and regroup, in the process sowing doubt and discord in its ranks.

Dingell envisioned a straightforward power play: He would ram a bill through the House, and then the Senate, backed by a coalition of Republicans and pressure from industry groups. The strategy suited him. An avid hunter, whose office is adorned with animal heads, Dingell is a large man, tall and physically imposing, who can intimidate his colleagues, much like Lyndon Johnson in the famous series of photographs by George Tames. Dingell took such delight in playing the heavy that he even coined a term for his technique. He called it "diddling." To diddle someone was to aggressively work them over in a very public way and keep going after them until they submitted. Once, while we worked on a bill together, I suggested getting on with business. "No, no," he replied. "I want to diddle that guy a little longer."

Dingell and I introduced competing measures to rewrite the Clean Air Act, though little doubt existed as to whose bill commanded more support. But both were referred to the Health and the Environment Subcommittee—so even though Dingell chaired the full committee, the chairman's powers initially lay with me.

As soon as the new administration settled in, I used those powers to hold oversight hearings intended to educate fellow members, Senate colleagues, and the public about the dire nature of what Reagan planned to do. Bill Dannemeyer, the subcommittee's ranking member, was an adversary from the outset. He didn't deny that pollution was a problem, Dannemeyer once told the committee, but he had started getting up earlier in the morning for his daily jog and that had made things much better.

One benefit of the close relationships my staff developed with the agencies was the willingness of some career employees to leak us information when they decided that the administration's plans were too reckless or damaging. Early on, someone at the Environmental Protection Agency leaked us Reagan's draft recommendations for amending the Clean Air Act, and the severe cuts he intended promptly became the basis for a hearing that aroused a public outcry.

Though Washington insiders may have thought that weakening the Clean Air Act was a fait accompli, the rest of the country was unpersuaded. A June 1981 Harris poll showed that 86 percent of Americans opposed the idea. When I invited Lou Harris, the pollster, to appear before the subcommittee, he announced that "clean air happens to be one of the sacred cows of the American people." Harris was hardly an authority on regulatory policy. But as an expert on public opinion he made a powerful witness nonetheless because he spoke directly to the fears of my congressional colleagues, an audience I very much wanted to influence. In mid-December, the bill had not budged, and industry was growing nervous. To a reporter's question about what was holding it up, GM's chief Washington lobbyist replied: "The Lou Harris poll."

By February, however, we could hold things back no longer and the steamroller moved on. Dingell's bill prevailed over mine, and the battle shifted to a series of counter-amendments, each designed to highlight a shortcoming, that my subcommittee colleagues and I introduced over the coming weeks. Dingell defeated every one of them—nearly sixty in all—usually by a 12–8 majority that consisted of three other Midwestern Democrats and the committee's Republicans.

Meanwhile, I employed a number of parliamentary tactics to throw sand in the gears, such as insisting that the committee clerk read the entire text of the bill aloud. In this way, we managed to slow matters to a crawl. With the 1982 midterm elections inching closer, Dingell came under growing pressure from nervous lawmakers. That pressure, and my delaying tactics, created considerable tension between the two of us. Then, in late March, a group of protesters leapt up in the middle of a subcommittee hearing and tore open their shirts to reveal "Dirty Dingell" T-shirts underneath. I was stunned, and quite unsure about the protocol for how a chairman should respond. As gently as possible, I suggested to the activists that their outburst was making it difficult to amend the bill, and politely but firmly asked them to stop. A few seats away, Dingell, fuming because I had not immediately evicted them, seemed to suspect that we were somehow in cahoots.

But the next day our amendment strategy had run its course, and Dingell's bill passed through subcommittee by a 13–7 vote. All that we had done had not stopped him.

WITH ACTION NOW SHIFTING TO THE FULL ENERGY AND COMMERCE Committee, which was under his chairmanship, our chances of stopping Dingell's bill appeared all but dead. We embarked on the same delaying tactics as before, in hopes that we could generate media and public attention. The House had something called a "Five-Minute Rule," which stipulated that committees could not meet for debate without first gaining unanimous consent on the floor. Each morning, the House clerk routinely waived the rule—until I started showing up to insist that he enforce it. Then I'd return to the committee and introduce a point of order that we didn't have permission to meet, thereby bringing everything to a halt. (The House eventually abolished this rule in large part, it's said, because of me.)

We also introduced in the full committee many of the amendments that had failed in subcommittee, still hoping to find an issue where we could prevail over Dingell and demonstrate that his strength was not as great as imagined. We needed a magic bullet. The only advantage in being an enormous underdog up against a broad and powerful coalition is that if you can find a way to weaken it at a critical moment sometimes the whole thing will fall apart. Three amendments struck us as promising, and these became critical test-case votes, recognized by everyone on the committee as important measures of strength.

On April 20, Colorado Democrat Tim Wirth introduced the first of these challenges, a measure moving up the date by which states would have to comply with clean air rules. We had chosen the Wirth amendment because it offered two attractive features. Regulatory jargon can be difficult to follow: MACT standards, PSDs, nonattainment provisions, and so on. But anyone can grasp the idea that no state would ever meet its obligation without a firm deadline. And because it did not affect a specific industry, the Wirth measure also served as an easy symbolic vote for members wishing to demonstrate their independence, which we hoped would be just enough to eke out a win.

The prospect of another Waxman-backed amendment did not exactly strike fear into our adversaries. Given that we had posted an uninterrupted losing streak now dozens of amendments long, nobody expected us to pass this one. But we stunned the Dingell coalition by prevailing, 22-19. Ralph Hall, the conservative Texas Democrat (who became a Republican), cast the deciding vote. He had never sided with us before, but he was persuaded to do so on this single amendment.

Shortly thereafter, Ron Wyden, an Oregon Democrat, followed with an amendment to undo a provision in the Dingell bill doubling the pollution permitted in national parks. This stood to be a much tougher vote because most of the pollution came from cars, and that put us on a collision course with the chairman himself. But Wyden was addressing an outrageous affront—one that was similarly easy for the public to grasp—and on April 28 it passed 25-13. Seeing his coalition coming apart, Dingell had no choice but to suspend the markup and regroup.

Throughout the summer, both sides prepared for the upcoming clash over the third test-case amendment, a provision limiting toxic air pollutants. The Wirth and Wyden amendments had shown that Dingell lacked the strength to force through anything he wanted. This one sought to go a step further and splinter his coalition. Imposing as the industries aligned against us were, they had come together on no firmer a basis than individual greed. The Reagan administration had promised each of them specific regulatory rollbacks. Our strategy was to muster all our strength to deny one industry its favors, and in doing so, set off a chain reaction—if one industry pulled out, others might waver, too, eventually turning the coalition members against one another. The idea was to prey upon industry paranoia that anyone left out of the bill would not only lose a cherished rollback, but probably face tougher restrictions than before to offset those that would be weakened elsewhere. Though the gathered interests operated in lockstep at the outset, all but the auto industry worried that Dingell might abandon them in a pinch.

We chose the toxic air amendment because the chemical industry had a great deal riding on the outcome. Two members whose constituents lived close to chemical plants, Jim Florio, a liberal Democrat from New Jersey, and Billy Tauzin, a conservative Democrat from Louisiana, agreed to sponsor the amendment. At issue was the question of how the law should classify thirty-seven substances that the EPA had identified as "potential carcinogens." The Florio-Tauzin amendment gave the agency four years to determine whether the substances were hazardous, and automatically listed them as such if no decision was made. Dingell's bill set a similar deadline, but with the key difference that it allowed the EPA to delay any final decision indefinitely, which had the practical effect of guaranteeing that it would.

As committee chairman, Dingell held the advantage of controlling the calendar and didn't have to call up the measure until he was certain that he had the votes to prevail. The call came in early August. Heading into markup, industry groups were brashly confident of a win. But I wasn't so sure. Over the summer, we had worked hard to organize a coalition, approaching members who, like Ralph Hall, did not ordinarily vote with us but might be persuaded to here. By my count, Florio-Tauzin hinged on a single vote—that belonging to Marc Marks, a Pennsylvania Republican.

Marks was an occasional vote for me on environmental issues, but as someone with industry in his district never a lock. He was a Jewish Republican, so we had religion in common, and I had come to know him as an honest and sincere fellow. But Marks was in a tough spot. Republicans pushed him around whenever he took moderate positions (he later switched parties), so I didn't expect to get him. But I knew that if we could peel him off, we stood a good chance to carry the day. Over the summer, Marks told me that he would do it.

But when Dingell recalled the committee after months of inactivity, we discovered that we could not get ahold of Marks— always an ominous sign. Everyone assumed the worst, and on the night before the vote, it looked to me like the end. The next morning, as we were about to begin, I approached him in the committee room. "Are you going to be with me?" I asked apprehensively. "Yes, I will," he replied. Behind me and just out of earshot, my chief of staff, Phil Schiliro, stood anxiously awaiting word. I leaned over and told him, "Don't smile, but he's with us." For a moment, I started choking up at the realization that all our effort on behalf of what had often seemed a hopeless cause was about to produce a win. On August 11,

1982, the Dingell amendment failed by Marks's single vote, and soon afterward Florio-Tauzin prevailed. An ashen-faced Dingell brought down his gavel and declared, "Meeting recessed."

With that unexpected loss, Reagan's historic endeavor to shred the Clean Air Act came to a sudden and ignominious end. Dingell lost the opportunity to revive his bill when his outside coalition collapsed. Its prize suddenly vanished, the chemical industry withdrew its support, and others soon followed, having lost confidence that they could prevail. American industry and the Reagan administration never mounted another such full-scale assault. But the act itself still needed updating. Having fought back efforts to weaken it, we now turned to the task of making it stronger.

IN BLOCKING REAGAN, WE PRESERVED THE LAW REQUIRING POL-luted areas to improve their air and clean areas to stay that way. But other problems lingered. Acid rain caused by Midwestern utilities burning high-sulfur Appalachian coal was killing lakes and forests in the Northeast and Canada. For several years running, the Senate's Environment and Public Works Committee had passed acid rain controls, but none ever made it to the Senate floor: Robert Byrd, the Democratic majority leader who represented the coal state of West Virginia, made sure of this. By 1983, however, Byrd had been relegated to the minority, and Republican margins in both houses had suffered in the midterm elections for Reagan's overreaching. Several of us in the House decided to take up acid rain.

Science showed clearly that acidic emissions from outdated power plants were the source of this menace. Fixing it would be an expensive proposition that required outfitting smoke-stacks with scrubbers—a cost that utilities were loath to bear, while Midwesterners feared it would drive their electric bills through the roof. Coal miners in the Midwest and Appalachia feared that switching to cleaner, low-sulfur coal, which was mined elsewhere, would cost them their jobs.

This regional dilemma caused the problem to persist: To one degree or another, everyone cared about acid rain. But only the Midwestern lawmakers who represented the offending utilities cared enough to fight to the death. To solve this regional problem, we set out to find a national solution that would spread the cost across the entire country. Doing so, we believed, would redistribute the main impediment to Midwestern cooperation—the cost of modernization—but in an easy enough way for the rest of us to bear that no one would object too strenuously. We settled on the idea of including a small add-on to electricity bills.

But before we could act, the administration threatened to upend the process. Citing an obscure provision in the 1977 Clean Air Act, Reagan's EPA administrator, Anne Burford, announced plans to impose harsh economic sanctions on 218 communities across the country that had failed to meet a 1982 deadline for clean air. Burford's legal interpretation was dubious, but her intention couldn't have been clearer. Were the sanctions enforced, cities and states would immediately deluge Congress with furious demands that the law be rewritten, quickly and loosely: industry's dream come true. (In a grim irony that no doubt doubled as an advantage to our opponents, the sanctions included forfeiture of federal grants for clean air programs.)

Politics indeed makes strange bedfellows. Having just fought to maintain one set of deadlines, it suddenly became imperative to extend another—and my yeoman ally turned out to be none other than Bill Dannemeyer. The key to political victory is always being open to unlikely alliances. Even someone with whom you're at odds 98 percent of the time—certainly the case here!—may still become a useful partner. Dannemeyer normally sided with industry, but his smog-choked Orange County district stood to get hammered with sanctions, which put us fleetingly on the same side.

Together we offered an amendment postponing the deadline to the fiscal appropriations bill moving through the House, and encountered the expected opposition. "The law is the law," argued Dingell, having long urged the EPA to enforce the sanctions. Amending the law required a vote of the full House. On June 2, 1983, the Dannemeyer-Waxman amendment passed 227-136. Reagan's gambit proved too blunt an instrument, and succumbed to regional politics: So many districts stood to lose that he could not assemble even the possibility of a majority.

Though we dodged that bullet, knotty regional issues were still tying up efforts to address acid rain. Later that month, I joined with Gerry Sikorski, a Minnesota Democrat, to introduce a bill requiring the dirtiest power plants in the country to install pollution control technology, of which the federal government would cover 90 percent of the cost through the electricity bill fee. Here was a proposal that went beyond merely "splitting the difference" and actually solved the acid rain problem equitably for all sides: It managed at once to preserve the environment, affordable utility rates, and high-sulfur coal jobs.

To build support, I convened a series of field hearings in the Midwest intended to showcase this winning proposition that delivered an environmental benefit without imposing the regional economic consequences Midwesterners had come to fear. Even though they stood to gain $3 billion in federal help, the utilities wanted no part of this, and relied on the White House to provide cover. In the face of overwhelming scientific consensus on the cause of acid rain, Reagan officials insisted that the jury was still out.

By the following spring, we believed that we had put together a narrow majority that, from the outside, wouldn't have appeared to make much sense. Every non-Midwestern Democrat on the subcommittee supported a bill that would tax their constituents to pay for pollution control in another part of the country. Opposing the idea were all six Republicans and three Midwestern Democrats. The remaining member, Dennis Eckart, an Ohio Democrat, stood to tip the balance, and his was ordinarily a solid vote for the environment. But unemployment from industrial closings had ravaged his district, which was also home to two of the fifty utility plants the bill targeted for clean-up. We had negotiated for weeks to earn his support, and, believing that we had it, I called for a vote—only to be stunned as Eckart sided with the opposition, striking down, by a single vote, the entire acid rain measure.

The next year we tried again, this time with provisions that would make it cheaper and easier for utilities to cut sulfur dioxide emissions. This time, the bill made it through subcommittee, but no further, after industry groups spent more money lobbying against it that any other measure that year. In the mid-1980s, clean air was an issue in transition. Industry's attempt to weaken regulations had failed; but it had not yet been compelled to accept stronger ones.

IN CONTRAST TO WHAT MANY PEOPLE IMAGINE, LEGISLATIVE DE-bates rarely occur within fixed parameters, or at least not for very long—the center is constantly moving. In the years it can take to pass a major piece of legislation like the Clean Air Act, the terms of debate often shift significantly. Sometimes the balance shifts gradually and by design, such as from a sustained lobbying effort. At other times, the shift happens suddenly and without warning, the consequence of a new president, a shake-up in Congress, or a major news event that recasts public opinion.

In the early morning hours of December 3, 1984, a Union Carbide pesticide plant in Bhopal, India, leaked forty tons of deadly methyl isocyanate gas, instantly killing more than three thousand people and maiming 100,000 more in one of the worst industrial disasters history has ever seen. The Bhopal tragedy riveted the world, and, practically overnight, turned public attention in the United States to the dangers of toxic air pollutants.

Our inadequate clean air laws provided plenty of cause for concern. Incredibly, the EPA did not consider methyl isocyanate a hazardous substance, nor other plainly dangerous chemicals like phosgene, although it had been used as a poison gas in World War I. At the time of the disaster, the agency recognized just five substances as toxic pollutants—a shortcoming the Florio-Tauzin amendment had sought to address two years earlier. But that effort had died with the 1982 bill.

EPA's haplessness in this area stemmed from the sort of bureaucratic breakdown of common sense that brings justified contempt upon the way government sometimes works. The agency's policy was not to list a substance as a toxic air pollutant until it was prepared to regulate it—but it also refused to regulate any substance not already recognized as a toxic air pollutant. Obviously, this circular logic prevented anything from ever being done. In the fourteen years since the Clean Air Act had come into being, the EPA had categorized only a handful of 650 chemicals as dangerous air pollutants.

A catastrophe like Bhopal creates unique conditions in which long dormant issues can suddenly find new life and rocket to the top of the congressional agenda—but it's important to move quickly. To capitalize on public concern, we held a field hearing the very next week in an auditorium located along the fence line of a Union Carbide plant in Institute, West Virginia, that produced methyl isocyanate. Greg Wetstone, an environmental counsel on my subcommittee staff, traveled ahead to interview local officials and other residents and gather information on the plant's safety procedures.

Greg's discoveries were troubling, even heartbreaking. Located in the narrow Kanawha Valley, the plant was identical to the one in Bhopal and emitted hazardous chemicals that appeared to pose the risk of a Bhopal-like incident. The plant manufactured another toxin called mercaptan, the gas additive responsible for the smell in your stove, which created overpowering odors that burned the eyes and lungs of those who lived nearby on the valley floor, forcing them indoors on windless days. These were the area's poorest residents, since the better-off could afford to live high in the hills, where the air was cleaner.

Public safety was an afterthought. Local cancer rates were 25 percent higher than the national average. One schoolteacher had taken to sleeping on an incline to prevent fluid from building in his lungs. At the hearing, a union representative testified that the evacuation plan was to "put a wet cloth over your face and go crosswind," only to be corrected by a school official who pointed out that a crosswind path in the valley would lead one into the Kanawha River on one side or up a mountain on the other. Residents were left to find solace in what they said was the company's assurance that "if you can smell it, it can't hurt you." As the community's largest employer, Union Carbide held tremendous sway, which discouraged many people from testifying. The reality that the company could ruin the local economy by relocating the plant was clear to municipal officials and workers alike.

Coming on the heels of Bhopal, the hearing drew enormous attention and became the lead story on every network news show. The few days we'd had to prepare for the hearing hadn't allowed for as thorough an investigation as would normally occur. But even the abbreviated effort produced startling revelations. Union Carbide had reported to state regulators that the Institute plant emitted twelve pounds of chemicals into the air each day. A scientist from the Occupational Safety and Health Administration testified that, in fact, the plant emitted 11,000 tons of toxic materials every year, including about sixty chemicals, many known carcinogens among them. As if to underscore the danger, an alarm from the plant sounded during the hearing, briefly throwing the proceedings into chaos, since no one knew if chemicals had leaked and if we had to run for our lives. (We later learned from a company memo that plant managers had feared that an accident could cause widespread casualties.)

OUR PURPOSE THAT DAY WAS NOT ONLY TO EXAMINE CHEMICAL plant safety, but to try and answer a fundamental question: Just how toxic was the air that Americans breathe? Before you can begin thinking about a legislative solution, you must first understand the scope of the problem.

We knew from EPA's failures that government did little to control the release of airborne pollutants. But we soon discovered an even more basic shortcoming that made quantifying the problem impossible: No one collected data about how many chemicals were released into the air each year—not federal, state, or local governments or even the chemical companies themselves. The EPA lacked such rudimentary information as an up-to-date list of the nation's chemical plants and where they were located.

Just as we had done with pharmaceutical companies when trying to understand the orphan drug issue, we initiated a broad voluntary survey of the country's largest chemical manufacturers to find out which toxic substances they put into the air. Only fifty of the eighty-six companies we approached supplied detailed data. But even these incomplete responses indicated that 80 million tons of toxic pollutants entered the air every year—far more than anyone had imagined.

In the wake of Bhopal, spewing carcinogens into the air was bad enough; but refusing to share basic safety information with government and worried neighbors was not just arrogant, but outright offensive. Citizens have a right to know when dangers lurk, even if their elected officials choose not to protect them. To ensure public awareness, I joined Gerry Sikorski, Tim Wirth and Jim Florio in proposing a national inventory of toxins that were known, or suspected to cause, cancer, birth defects, and other chronic health problems. In addition to giving people the right to know what chemicals their local plants were producing, the bill granted anyone injured by poisonous releases the right to sue in federal court, and also required the EPA to regulate more airborne pollutants. We attached the amendment to a hazardous waste clean-up bill moving through the House.

By the time our amendment came before the full House on December 10, 1985, it had been stripped of everything but the Toxic Release Inventory. The inventory did nothing to limit emissions or impose a single new cost—it simply established a way to measure airborne pollution. But the Chemical Manufacturers Association, the industry trade group, virulently opposed even this much, and claimed that our survey's estimate of the 80 million tons of pollution wildly exaggerated the true amount.

Industry groups and their allies launched a full-court press to induce panic and whip up opposition. Republican congressmen claimed that the measure would force hardware stores, gas stations, and beauty parlors to document which chemicals they release. But still we prevailed by the narrowest of margins, 212-211, and early the next year the concept became law.

By the end of 1986, the Clean Air Act appeared no closer

to renewal, the problem of acid rain was getting worse, and the EPA still would not regulate more than a handful of hazardous substances. But beneath the surface, the debate was moving our way, and we could now claim a tangible legislative achievement. The National Toxic Release Inventory could not, of course, reduce air pollution. But the invaluable information it provided became the basis for legislation that could. The first report appeared in March 1989 and immediately became front-page news across the country: It showed that a staggering *2.7 billion pounds* of toxic air pollution was released into the air in 1987.

Though it wasn't clear at the time, the turning point in the decade-long battle for clean air occurred during the next session of Congress, in another showdown over deadlines. Air quality sanctions due to take effect on the last day of the year, December 31, 1987, convinced many in Washington that an agreement had to be near. House negotiations opened in July, but after several months it became clear that not even the impending deadline would force a resolution.

With sanctions set to strike nearly every urban area, focus shifted to postponement. Industry and its allies favored a two-year extension that would effectively remove any pressure on Congress to act promptly. I considered this pressure valuable motivation, and with Silvio Conte, a Massachusetts Republican, offered an amendment extending the deadline by just eight months. Since the competing provisions required a floor vote, this soon shaped up as the first measure of House sentiment toward clean air in several years, and a defining test of strength.

The day before the vote, Dingell and John Murtha, a formidable Democratic congressman from Pennsylvania, took the unusual step of predicting that their side would win handily. This threw us, since our count showed us winning narrowly. When voting began the next day, Dingell and Murtha looked on in dismay as presumed allies began to go our way, just a few at first, and then, as the outcome became clear, a stampede that ultimately gave us a ninety-five-vote margin—and a ringing declaration of where Congress now stood.

This resounding defeat of those who had held the upper hand for so long sent a shockwave through Washington. Everyone suddenly realized that the forces of industry had badly overestimated the willingness of many members, especially Northeastern Republicans, to go on record against the environment. Absent a pressing local reason to do so, most simply didn't see the need.

The psychological advantage we gained from this victory drove the subsequent debate. Dingell had strength enough in committee to defeat us on most days. But we had prevailed in all three votes of the full House—on the Dannemeyer-Waxman amendment, the Toxic Release Inventory, and now the eight-month extension. The vision of ramming it through no longer an option, Dingell and his allies began to doubt whether they could still prevail if a measure went to the floor. Industry confidence began to collapse.

Throughout the next year the Energy and Commerce Committee negotiated toward a broad overhaul of the Clean Air Act. Though our opponents had become more interested in resolving issues than in battling them out, we could not reach agreement before Congress adjourned. But our disappointment did not last long.

IN 1989, OUTSIDE EVENTS CONSPIRED ONCE AGAIN TO JERK THE debate even further in our direction. In Washington, Ronald Reagan gave way to George H. W. Bush, who bid to distinguish himself from his predecessor by declaring that he would be "the environmental president" and promising to renew the Clean Air Act. George Mitchell of Maine replaced Robert Byrd of

West Virginia as Senate majority leader, instantly transforming the fight over acid rain: The Senate's leading Democrat became someone whose constituents suffered, rather than prospered, from the regulatory status quo. Beyond Washington, the effects of weak environmental laws were coming into visibility everywhere. Needles and other medical waste started washing up on the Jersey Shore. The first report from the National Toxic Registry Index appeared, laying waste to the industry claim that severe air pollution was not a problem. And then, on March 24, 1989, the Exxon *Valdez* tanker disaster spilled 11 million gallons of oil into Prince William Sound, killing most wildlife and poisoning miles of pristine Alaskan coastline.

Despite claims of environmental commitment, President Bush and his administration came up with a revision of the Clean Air Act that was still weaker than what we wanted. He nevertheless did us a tremendous service by declaring the environment a presidential priority and submitting his own bill—he put his reputation on the line, which greatly increased the chance that some version of the Clean Air Act would become law. Our job became taking his bill and rewriting it to match his lofty rhetoric.

Using the Bush bill as our vehicle, rather than introduce a competing measure, we scheduled a series of hearings to highlight its major deficiencies and lay the groundwork for strengthening amendments. Momentum had swung to our side, but there remained countless ways for our opponents to weaken a bill so that the law wouldn't have its intended effects—in some cases, a single word change was enough to do the trick.

As we prepared to debate Bush's bill, a contact in the EPA leaked my staff an earlier draft of the plan that enabled us to compare the two, and see where and how the final product had been diluted. The original Clean Air Act of 1970 established the EPA administrator's role under the law in unam-

biguous language: It was written that he or she "shall" carry
out the enumerated duties. The early Bush draft maintained
this language—but the final version swapped "shall" for "may,"
thereby introducing the possibility that a future EPA administrator, should he or she so desire, "may" choose *not* to enforce
the law.

Bush selected as his first EPA administrator William Reilly,
a moderate environmentalist, whom we summoned before the
subcommittee to explain this curious choice of word. Reilly
insisted that he had every intention of enforcing the law to its
fullest extent. But we kept pressing him: Why the tricky language? He finally conceded that he could not explain it. (More
likely he could, but chose not to.) Reilly later admitted to me
that while our grilling had been tough, what bothered him
most about the hearing was that none of his fellow Republicans had spoken up in his defense. None was familiar enough
with the bill's details to argue over them.

By now, our clean air agenda had grown to encompass four
parts: acid rain, smog, toxic air pollutants, and a new issue,
ozone depletion. Scientists warned that the hole in the earth's
atmospheric ozone layer would have serious climatic consequences were it allowed to continue growing. Fixing the problem entailed reducing the amount of man-made ozone-depleting
chemicals called chlorofluorocarbons (CFCs), which meant
changing industrial manufacturing processes. This drew opposition from the usual quarters. At one memorable proceeding,
Bill Dannemeyer proposed building giant fans that would blow
ozone up into the stratosphere. But few any longer doubted
that there would be major improvements in the law.

During the 1980s, Congress came to consider more and
more environmental provisions that were undesirable from an
industry standpoint. And each year the proposals grew stronger. Everyone now had something to fear: Smog standards hit

automakers, acid rain measures hit utilities and coal, toxic emission limits hit chemical companies, and CFC restrictions hit appliance manufacturers. The likelihood that Congress would finally mandate tougher air standards compelled each of these interests to rethink its strategy. Reductions had to come from somewhere—therefore any breaks given to one industry came at the expense of the others. Business interests that had once moved in lockstep now began looking out for themselves.

This was precisely the opposite dynamic to that of 1982, when everyone lined up behind Dingell. Back then, we targeted industries like chemical manufacturing because we didn't have the strength to take on President Reagan and Dingell directly. But with every industry now fighting to deny breaks to the rest, Dingell and the automakers no longer held such a strong hand. We decided to try our luck and go right after them. If we could beat Dingell and set tough standards for automobile emissions, we wagered that he would be more inclined to compromise on everything else. In September, when the time came to decide on amendments, I engineered an early showdown on a measure I'd introduced setting strict tailpipe standards.

Like so many of our previous fights, this one looked to be close. To ensure that no one missed its overriding significance, and to pressure members to vote with us, I took to describing it as "the environmental vote of the decade," a characterization that the press eagerly adopted. To rattle industry, I told reporters that I expected the "real" fight to come on the House floor, where Dingell had not fared well, while behind the scenes, we set to work trying to take away some of his support.

The struggle came down to two members ordinarily inclined toward him. Tom Tauke, an Iowa Republican, worried that stricter emission standards would hurt his district—his concern was not over autos, however, but over tractors and other farm equipment that fell under the same standard. By assuring him that they would not be singled out for tougher requirements, we were able to bring him along. Ralph Hall, the conservative Democrat from Texas, had balked at what he perceived to be overambitious limits on auto emissions. One way in which Congress worked to reduce pollution was by setting requirements and letting industry develop the technology to meet them, a mechanism known as "technology forcing standards." This is how the catalytic converter, among other innovations, was brought into being. The automakers routinely claimed that they couldn't possibly meet our proposed standards, though most experts believed that they could. We walked Hall through the amendment, section by section, explaining why our goals were feasible, and how, in the event that they turned out not to be, the EPA would be permitted to adjust the standards later on. Satisfied by what we told him, he approached Dingell in an anteroom just off the committee chambers. "John," he said, "I think Henry's got something here." This is a congressman's way of conveying that he intends to support something—and by doing so, Hall also gently told Dingell that he was going to lose the fight.

For more than a decade, Dingell and I had battled ferociously over the Clean Air Act, and we had often tried to get him to sit down and work out a deal. Dingell never budged, and so neither did I, each of us believing that we would prevail when matters came to a vote. Seeing that this was now unlikely to happen on the issue so important to him, Dingell did what any good congressman would do, and sat down to negotiate the best possible deal for his constituents. Two hours later, we had settled on the outline of an agreement. Most importantly, our agreement was "through conference," meaning that no changes could be made in conference with the Senate unless all parties agreed, which made success seem all the more likely.

The other members of the House were thunderstruck by the

news—the deal had seemingly come out of the blue. "We had thought it would be King Kong versus Godzilla," Jim Cooper, a Tennessee Democrat, remarked afterward. But everyone recognized, with a mix of relief and excitement, that the long campaign for clean air had passed what had sometimes appeared an insurmountable obstacle. When Dingell and I reached across the conference table to formally shake hands on the agreement, the committee room burst into loud applause.

FROM THERE, THE BILL FOLLOWED A SLOW BUT STEADY PATH TO the president. Having struck a deal on auto emissions, Dingell and I had every incentive to find further agreements so that we could continue to be together. The negotiations carried on after the subcommittee reported the bill to the full committee, and by the following spring a broad overhaul of the Clean Air Act had taken shape.

The struggle over acid rain between the Midwest and the rest of the country continued to be a major source of contention. Only a series of marathon negotiating sessions bought a settlement. One of the longest, to hammer out an acid rain compromise, began on the morning of April 4 and dragged on for thirty-four mind-numbing hours. "You know the difference between being in a medium-security prison and being in Congress?" mused Illinois Democrat Terry Bruce during a break. "There isn't any. In both facilities you can walk around all you want—you just can't leave."

Late the next evening, our business finally complete, the bleary-eyed members of the Energy and Commerce Committee voted 42-1 (Bill Dannemeyer dissenting) to move the clean air bill onto the House floor, and a few weeks later, the House overwhelmingly ratified our work 401-21.

Dingell was practically wistful. "We negotiated rather than fought," he told reporters. "It's a process with which I am not entirely comfortable, but it has been a success. It is a good piece of legislation." I shared his sentiments.

The Bush administration made a key strategic miscalculation that wound up strengthening the law considerably in the final stages of negotiation. Bush officials played an active role in negotiating the Senate bill, but not its House counterpart. Assuming that a weaker bill would emerge from the House, White House negotiators had insisted that the Senate agreement bind its participants only through the floor vote, and not through the subsequent House-Senate conference, as Dingell and I had agreed to do. By freeing senators to vote as they wished, the administration expected that they would combine the weakest elements of both bills into the final legislation. Instead, with an election looming, they supported the strongest provisions in both bills, producing a law that was much better than either the House or Senate drafts had been.

With little choice, President Bush signed the Clean Air Act Amendments into law on November 15, 1990.

THE CLEAN AIR ACT AMENDMENTS OF 1990 WERE THE OUTCOME of one of the longest, most scrutinized, and hardest fought legislative battles that Washington had witnessed in decades. But that effort yielded a law that ranks as one of Congress's historic achievements.

Five years after its passage, more than half the U.S. cities that exceeded urban smog standards had come into compliance. Production of ozone-depleting chemicals had dropped by more than 90 percent. Power plant emissions that cause acid rain fell to half their 1980 levels, and at a fraction of the cost industry had predicted. Cancer-causing toxic emissions decreased by 1.6 billion tons annually, a drop of more than 25 percent. The EPA's meager list of five hazardous air pollutants expanded to 189, including such potentially lethal substances as dioxin, mercury, and methyl isocyanate, the chemical that destroyed Bhopal. When fully implemented, the law will prevent tens of thousands of premature deaths, tens of thousands of hospital admissions for respiratory and cardiovascular illnesses, and millions of lost workdays each year.

Some of the greatest successes have come in the most contentious area of debate. In 1989, Ford Motor Company executives testified that "we just do not have the technology to comply" with new tailpipe standards. Yet within four years automakers managed to do just that, and the controversial "technology forcing standards" triggered development of sophisticated engine-control equipment that produced lower pollution, more power, and greater fuel economy. Today's typical new car is twenty times cleaner than a comparable model in 1981, and hybrids like Ford's Escape are forty to fifty times as much. In fact, automakers met with relative ease the ambitious standards they once claimed would destroy jobs and cast the economy into recession—the law worked so well that it quickly became hard to recall what all the fuss had been about.

The Clean Air Act offers several lessons. The first, and most important, is that success is possible even against overwhelming opposition. What began as a seemingly unstoppable assault on a landmark law ended with the enactment of the strongest environmental legislation in American history. The entire battle unfolded while Republicans controlled the White House. Despite fierce opposition throughout, the 1990 measure was stronger in almost every respect than the bills debated in the 1980s. And in the end, even Godzilla and King Kong came together.

The second lesson is that while industry claims often frame the debate, they are usually exaggerated, not accurate descriptions of the truth but tactics to stop unwanted measures, regardless of need or merit. Many business interests predicted catastrophe were the law enacted. DuPont Chemical warned of "severe economic and social disruption," and Mobil "severe supply chain disruptions" for gasoline. But no one rioted, the economy grew, and Americans never had a problem filling up their tanks.

This is true largely because of the third lesson: Good legislation works as intended. The Clean Air Act passed only after years of oversight hearings, which had singled out the worst problems and the best solutions, and after intense debate over how it was to be drafted had accounted for the concerns of all sides. Rather than split the difference, the focus stayed fixed on the goal of achieving clean air in a way that would work for everyone—and earned the bill broad support from both parties as a result. Because it was so carefully designed, the Clean Air Act has stood up to subsequent White House efforts to weaken it and industry lawsuits challenging it. Today, it stands as testimony that Congress can still find ways to dramatically improve the quality of everyone's life and well-being that serve citizens and businesses alike.

CHAPTER 6

Nutrition Labeling and Dietary Supplements

IN THE MID-1980S, A HEALTH CRAZE SWEPT THE COUNTRY. For the first time, large numbers of Americans became aware of the importance of proper diet and exercise to good health, and in an effort to prevent heart disease, strokes, and cancer, many tried to cut down on their intake of cholesterol and sodium. More than most new national enthusiasms, this one reached Congress. One reason may have been that we were always the first to see reports on public health, like the ones issued during this period linking sodium and hypertension. But my own hunch is that the profile of those most at risk bore an uncanny resemblance to the members of the U.S. Congress: paunchy, middle-aged-and-older men whose diets and health regimens would not have elicited the surgeon general's approval.

As someone who has always battled weight problems and dieted constantly, I was no exception. Along with some colleagues, I started making regular visits to the House gym, and over the years have tried to stick with a program. I've discovered that staying healthy has more in common with legislating that one might imagine: Both demand years of perseverance and effort without any assurance that the payoff will resemble anything like what you had originally envisioned. And as the chairman of the House subcommittee on health, I was more acutely aware than most of my shortcomings in this area.

One frustration soon encountered by anyone trying to watch his diet in those days was the difficulty of finding even basic nutritional information about most foods—information like calories, sodium, and cholesterol content. Food manufacturers had a spotty record of what they chose to reveal on product labels, if they chose to reveal anything at all. No law required them to do so. Some products offered comprehensive nutritional details, some only limited information, and others nothing at all. The result was haphazard and confusing. Recognizing a marketing opportunity in the new awareness about diet, food manufacturers started including health claims on their labels ("Low Cholesterol!"), while simultaneously downplaying or ignoring important information that might discourage sales of a product, such as high levels of fat and sodium. This made life even harder for health-conscious consumers: No one could make sense of the labels. Anyone attempting to watch what he ate, including many congressmen, soon realized that he could not really do so until food makers began providing basic nutritional information.

By the end of Ronald Reagan's presidency, the problem of food labeling had grown acute, owing not only to the inconsistency of what was being disclosed but also to the administration's passion for deregulation, which created the additional problem of exaggerated and misleading health claims. The trouble began with a breakfast cereal, Kellogg's All-Bran. In 1984, Kellogg's launched a multimillion-dollar marketing campaign for All-Bran that included the claim, printed in bold letters on the cereal box, "The National Cancer Institute believes a high fiber, low fat diet may reduce your risk of some kinds of cancer." Kellogg's repeated the claim in full-page ads in major Sunday newspapers and magazines. This was the first time a company had ever claimed a direct link between a food product and cancer prevention, and the implied endorsement of a highly respected governmental medical organization like the National Cancer Institute caused sales of All-Bran to skyrocket. Other cereal makers quickly responded with claims of their own.

Since 1906, federal policy had held that any product claiming to treat or prevent disease had to be tested and regulated as a drug. All-Bran had not been, so the ad campaign appeared to violate federal rules. The Food and Drug Administration, which oversees the safety of the country's food, considered stopping the ads and even seizing boxes of All-Bran, until Reagan appointees intervened and let Kellogg's continue.

This touched off a stampede among food makers to issue ever more aggressive and outlandish claims about the nutritional benefits of their products, claims that were often misleading and soon lost any grounding in scientific fact. Skippy touted its peanut butter as having "less sugar than other leading national brands," but its label didn't state how much sugar Skippy contained. Del Monte claimed its canned vegetables were as nutritious as fresh ones, but didn't mention that they contain three hundred times as much sodium. Campbell's Soup did away with specifics altogether and began referring to itself as "health insurance," though its products, too, contained staggering amounts of sodium.

In many cases, the clear intention was to deceive consumers. Bertolli Extra Light Olive Oil may have looked like a healthy, low-calorie product—that was certainly the idea—but its "light" claim derived not from a calorie count, but from the color of the olive oil itself. Sara Lee Light Classics French Cheesecake boasted "only 200 calories per serving," even though a serving contained *more* calories than Sara Lee's regular cheesecake. Confronted by an FDA task force, the company claimed the term "light" referred to the cheesecake's texture. Wonder Lite Bread boasted that it contained "no cholesterol," without noting that few types of bread contain any cholesterol whatsoever. Food manufacturers scrambling to cash in on the health trend wanted only to convince consumers that such products were good for them—even when they were not. Simply claiming to be healthy usually got people to buy them.

JOE MOAKLEY, A MASSACHUSETTS DEMOCRAT WHOSE FAMILY HAD A history of hypertension, became the first member of Congress to try to elicit standard nutritional information when he introduced a bill requiring food makers to disclose sodium content on their product labels. Jim Cooper, a Tennessee Democrat, twice put forth a Lite Food Labeling Act that would have defined "light" as meaning "one-third the calories, fat or sodium that would be in the food without alteration." Both measures died after manufacturers complained that the requirement would impose too great a cost, confuse people with too much new information, and, for a host of other specious reasons, could not possibly be made to work. In Congress, the most commonsense ideas are often the ones that draw the most heated protests.

There is an inherent tension to the subject of government regulation that centers on knowing when it is necessary for the government to intervene and when it is not. How does Congress know if it has gone too far or hasn't gone far enough? My own belief is that people always deserve whatever information is necessary to make responsible decisions, especially about important matters of health. If government decides not to regulate such matters, it ought to provide the information and let consumers decide for themselves. Food labeling was clearly an area where government needed to play a role, first in establishing a way for consumers to get basic nutritional information, and second in stopping the spread of dangerous and misleading health claims.

By the time Reagan left office, even some food manufacturers had begun to realize the need for federal labeling standards. By the late 1980s, the FDA had descended into chaos, the result of a toxic combination of factors, including severe budget cuts under Reagan imposed even as the agency's responsibilities were multiplying and pressure on it mounting to approve drugs faster, due largely to the exploding AIDS epidemic. Agency morale was at a historic low. The Reagan administration had undermined enforcement of many basic food and drug laws, and then, in 1989, the FDA was rocked by scandal and Commissioner Frank Young forced to resign after several officials were convicted for falsifying safety and effectiveness data for drugs that the agency had approved. The crisis was such that President George H. W. Bush, encouraged by Republican senator Orrin Hatch, nominated as his FDA commissioner Dr. David Kessler, a tough, enforcement-minded pediatrician and lawyer (and former Hatch aide) who had taught food and drug law at Columbia Law School.

The trouble from an industry standpoint was that when the Reagan administration stopped enforcing the laws, many state attorneys general stepped into the void, suing companies like Campbell's, for claiming its soup decreases the risk of heart disease, and Kellogg's, for claiming that Frosted Flakes made a healthier snack than bananas, oranges, or apples. The threat that any number of states could take action fostered enormous uncertainty among food manufacturers. No one was entirely sure about what was or was not permitted under the law.

It fell to me, as chairman of the subcommittee responsible for overseeing public health, to try and remedy these short-comings. In July 1989, I introduced a bill proposing the Nutrition Labeling and Education Act (NLEA), which required all processed foods to carry labels listing the amount of calories, saturated and unsaturated fat, cholesterol, sodium, complex carbohydrates, sugar, protein, and dietary fiber. The bill also established uniform federal definitions of terms like "light," "lean," and "low fat," and stipulated that any claims of disease prevention had to be backed by "significant scientific agreement" rather than just the wishes of the marketing department. Our intention was to make the law as comprehensive as possible, so that ultimately every food product, including fresh fruit, vegetables, meat, and poultry, would carry nutritional information.

Unlike many other legislative efforts, this one did not sort out neatly along party lines. Food industry trade groups like the Grocery Manufacturers of America and the National Food Processors Association opposed the bill, particularly its curb on health claims. And though Republicans are usually attentive to what industry desires, here some were not. Louis Sullivan, the secretary of health and human services in the new George H. W. Bush administration, declared, "The grocery store has become a Tower of Babel, and consumers need to be linguists, scientists, and mind readers to understand the many labels they encounter." Ed Madigan of Illinois, the health subcommittee's ranking member, also liked the idea and agreed to work with us on legislation.

Having the support of the committee's top Republican created a collaborative, rather than an adversarial, process that limited what industry groups could do to stop the bill. At an

August hearing on the legislation, food industry representatives argued against a new law on grounds that it would be too costly and difficult to implement. The real reason they opposed it, which they couldn't air publicly, was that many of the products touted as "healthy" were clearly not so, and they worried that educated consumers would stop buying them. But Madigan's inclination toward the idea prevented them from pressing this claim too strongly even in private, since they required his goodwill in many other areas. In October, the bill passed the subcommittee on a voice vote.

Sensing that they could not kill the legislation, the industry groups switched tactics and instead sought to use the bill as a vehicle to escape state food safety requirements, a long-standing desire of their members. Their primary focus became ensuring that any new federal law would preempt a California measure known as Proposition 65, which required warning labels to be placed on any foods that contain a carcinogen. California voters had passed what was formally the Safe Drinking Water and Toxic Enforcement Act of 1986 as a ballot initiative to protect themselves from toxins. Food manufacturers hated the law because it presented them the choice of eliminating, at some cost, even trace amounts of carcinogens or else slapping a label on their product that read, "WARNING: This product contains chemicals known to the State of California to cause cancer and birth defects or other reproductive harm." The less than robust sales potential for carcinogenic foods prompted most manufacturers to ensure that whatever they sold in California was free of hazardous substances—in other words, Proposition 65 worked exactly as intended.

Not every legislative battle is decided in a dramatic showdown on the House floor. Some are won quietly through the clever drafting of a bill, and victory seized before the matter can ever come to a vote. This became our strategy. Despite the country's newfound interest in health and fitness, there was hardly a public clamor for better nutrition labeling, and none at all to preempt state food safety laws, except among industry trade groups. Consequently, few congressmen or senators felt strongly enough about the matter to spend political capital defending these laws—they simply didn't resonate with their constituents in nearly the same way as issues like clean air and tobacco. No groundswell was going to arise in our defense.

This meant that while many members were inclined toward our bill, they would also be willing to give away a great deal to achieve compromise. What food makers most wanted was to preempt Proposition 65, and there was reason to believe they might get their wish. Though Ed Madigan supported our push for uniform nutritional labeling, he made clear that he would support the industry's desire to override Proposition 65. So from the outset we anticipated that Madigan, or some other Republican, would put that option before the committee by introducing an amendment—and we doubted our ability to defeat it.

But winning a vote is not the only way to stop an amendment. Should a chairman determine that an amendment is not germane to the bill before his committee, he will rule the amendment out of order and dismiss it. With the nutritional labeling measure headed to full committee, its chairman, John Dingell, would be the one to decide.

Once we had identified the likeliest threat, we set about plotting to avoid it. Here was a situation where a thorough knowledge of the rules and deft use of language could work wonders. When Bill Corr, from the subcommittee staff, had sat down to draft the bill, he had in mind the possibility that there might arise a germaneness argument over an amendment to preempt Proposition 65, and had devised a clever linguistic trick to counter it. He wrote the Nutrition Labeling and Education Act to pertain specifically to "nutrients" rather than "food." The distinction might at first appear puzzling—until one remembers that "food" can contain both "nutrients" and "carcinogens," and therefore an amendment concerning carcinogens, such as any that would repeal Proposition 65, might not be germane to a bill dealing only with nutrients. In effect, the bill set a trap for our opponents.

The authority on germaneness, and other matters of rule and precedent, was the House parliamentarian. The job of parliamentarian is believed to have originated in 1857, when Speaker James L. Orr of South Carolina appointed a "messenger" named Thaddeus Morrice whose knack for remembering Orr's decisions made him an invaluable repository of institutional knowledge. Over the decades, others filled the role, and in 1927 Congress formalized the nonpartisan Office of the Parliamentarian, and later published a multivolume compendium of House precedents. Today, the parliamentarian is the figure who sits just to the right of the speaker whenever the House is in session, and holds enormous power in this capacity. It is the parliamentarian who reads the thousands of bills, resolutions, and executive communications introduced in the House each year; who decides which committee or committees those bills are referred to; and who commands unrivaled authority as an expert on all matters of legislative procedure and detail—including whether or not a nutrition bill could be drafted in such a way that a chairman might find cause to dismiss an amendment concerning carcinogens. With chairmen, as with everyone else, the opinion of the House parliamentarian carries great sway.

The value of having this nonpartisan arbiter was not, I must confess, initially clear to me. When, as a new congressman, I first encountered some obstacle in a rule, I appealed to Tip O'Neill, the ultimate authority as House speaker, to decide in my favor. In the California Assembly, the speaker determined the rules, and Jesse Unruh had maintained power by routinely using them in exactly the partisan fashion I envisioned. But O'Neill deferred to the parliamentarian and declined my entreaty. It came as a surprise to me that Tip O'Neill, the leader of my own party, couldn't just make the decision. But later on, when the Republicans gained control of the House, I came to appreciate the importance of having an honest broker to follow the rules. In the meantime, I drew a lesson from what I'd observed. Since having the speaker on your side is a great advantage, and the speaker always consulted the parliamentarian on issues of rules, it occurred to me that the parliamentarian held tremendous power that I might use to gain an edge. My staff and I became devoted students, consulting the parliamentarian on all matter of law and procedure, mastering the rules in our own right, and eventually pioneering, with his guidance, all sorts of legislative tactics and maneuvers.

When consulted about the drafting of the NLEA, the parliamentarian agreed that the distinction between nutrients and carcinogens was a meaningful one, and he ruled in our favor. This was a great advantage, for it enabled us, if the expected amendment on Proposition 65 materialized, to introduce a point of order and seek to have the amendment dismissed on grounds that it wasn't germane. But invoking such a ruling can sometimes involve an elaborate pas de deux. Though influential, the parliamentarian's ruling is an advisory opinion that ultimately takes a back seat to the decision of the chairman or speaker. While it's important to have, letting it be known that you have it is something of a delicate matter. I couldn't very well announce it before the committee, since doing so would openly challenge Dingell's authority, with whom we were then in the midst of the heated final stages of the Clean Air Act struggle and not on the friendliest of terms. Instead, my staff discreetly conveyed to his that we'd raised the question and the ruling had gone our way.

In May, Dingell called the bill for markup, and, sure enough, Madigan introduced an amendment directed at Proposition 65. I immediately made a point of order and explained the crucial distinction between nutrients and carcinogens. I never found out whether Dingell himself learned of the parliamentarian's ruling, but he gave every outward appearance of making up his own mind on the matter, right there before the committee. With theatrics befitting a powerful chairman, Dingell called for a dictionary, and an aide wheeled out one of the largest I had ever laid eyes on. Dingell looked up "nutrient" and read the definition aloud to the committee, then riffled through the pages until he got to "carcinogen" and did the same. That seemed to satisfy him. He dismissed the amendment after a brief debate, and our bill, thankfully intact, moved out of committee by another voice vote.

Having dodged the most serious attack on the bill's substance, we switched gears from defense to offense, and turned to the challenge of steering it the rest of the way through Congress. Though we looked to be in fine shape in the House, our concern was the Senate, and the possibility that industry trade groups might block it there. Senator Howard Metzenbaum, an Ohio Democrat, had introduced a measure similar to ours that had stalled in committee. Because senators have the power to place a hold on a bill, it is much easier to stop legislation in the Senate—outside groups need only convince one of them to do so.

Once the bill had passed the House Energy and Commerce Committee, we decided to sit down with representatives from several of the largest trade groups and see if we could strike a deal. Both sides had concerns that impelled them to the negotiating table. The food industry had three options: try to stop the bill, live with it as it was, or accept that something would pass and try to negotiate concessions in exchange for withdrawing opposition or even supporting the compromise. From our standpoint, the strong support in both chambers did not guarantee that a bill would make it through the Senate. Striking a compromise on the House bill, however, would all but assure victory in the Senate, since the industry groups would be ethically bound to honor any agreement they struck now. As summer arrived, both sides plunged into weeks of negotiations.

RESIGNED TO THE IMPENDING LABELING STANDARDS AND LIMITS on health claims, the food industry returned to the issue of preemption. Undermining Proposition 65 was, of course, out of the question; but disparities between FDA and state labeling standards remained a costly headache, from which manufacturers now sought relief. Whenever state requirements differed from federal standards, companies had to tailor their packaging to a niche market. Rectifying this struck me as a reasonable enough request. With the Nutrition Labeling and Education Act poised to supply the information consumers needed, the patchwork of state standards was no longer a necessary bulwark.

But reaching compromise required more than just winning me over. First in the House, and later in the Senate, a series of obscure region-specific obstacles had to be overcome to placate lawmakers or industries that might block a deal. Most people imagine Congress as grappling over weighty matters of state, but it is not always so. Our first challenge was Vidalia onions. Unbeknownst to me, these pungent little bulbs, a vital component of certain popular Southern cocktails, are often sold in liquor stores. Roy Rowland of Georgia did not think it fair that liquor stores, which do not offer much in the way of foodstuffs *besides* Vidalia onions, be required to post food labels solely to apprise their clientele of the nutritional merits of cocktail onions. We granted an exemption.

The next hitch was small mom-and-pop vegetable stands, which couldn't easily comply with the proposed labeling standards. These, too, earned an exemption.

The Senate demands seemed similarly arbitrary, though important to rectify given a senator's ability to stop a bill. One of the many federal-state disparities was the legal standard for what constitutes maple syrup. The FDA required a product to contain at least 80 percent maple syrup in order to be labeled as such. But Vermont, which regards maple syrup in the same way Germans regard beer, had a standard of 100 percent that was evidently a matter of ferocious state pride—Senator Jim Jeffords of Vermont threatened to block the legislation unless an exception were made for Vermont maple syrup. We relented to avoid that sticky situation.

A trickier impasse was whether dietary supplements would be subject to the bill's constraints on health claims. Senator Orrin Hatch of Utah, home to many of the largest supplement manufacturers, insisted there be separate—and more lenient— standards, since claims to prevent or cure disease are the primary reason most people take dietary supplements. Here we were not willing to concede because supplements were largely unregulated and in many cases posed a real danger to users' health. To save the bill, we agreed to insert a provision that directed the FDA to adopt a standard and procedure for evaluating and approving claims on dietary supplements, and to issue a binding recommendation one year after the law's enactment.

The most vexing problem, however, turned out to be candy. To prevent unscrupulous manufacturers from burying information in microscopic type, the bill stipulated that nutrition labels must be a certain size. A box of Milk Duds could simply print the label on the outside of the package. But a box of assorted candies could not, since each variety differed in nutritional content. Nor could the manufacturer adhere to the law by labeling individual candy wrappers without running afoul of the size requirement. Here was a problem that, I'll concede, none of us had foreseen. But it was of gravest concern to the Chocolate Manufacturers Association, and therefore needed addressing. Trade groups are unusually well funded and possess a hair-trigger willingness to try to block legislation they opposed. We could imagine the ads: "Congress is trying to take away your candy!" With some effort, we crafted a fix for variegated boxed candy.

Strange as it sometimes can be, haggling over obscure particulars is not at all unusual in the latter stages of the legislative process. Even sensible, well-written bills can't possibly anticipate every contingency, and there will always be a good case for making certain exceptions. The art of legislating is figuring out how to accommodate them without undermining the larger purpose. This can be difficult. No matter the issue, outside groups always tend toward purist positions. But for the legislative process to work, lawmakers need to make compromises that outside allies dislike. Some of the public interest groups that had been instrumental in bringing the issue of food safety to the fore opposed any deal preempting state standards. But to my mind, the benefits of doing so outweighed their objections. After several arduous weeks, we struck a deal.

One of the amazing things about legislation is that you can rewrite an entire bill in the middle of the process, which is what we did with the House measure between the committee and the floor vote, adding the concessions for candy, Vidalia onions, and some other odds and ends. We moved to place the bill on the suspension calendar, a fast-tracking system in which legislation that at least two-thirds of House members support is voted on with limited debate and no allowance for amend-ments. In late July, the House passed the measure by a voice vote, sent it on to the Senate, which tackled maple syrup and a few other issues, and we finally passed the joint version in late October. On November 8, 1990, President Bush signed the Nutrition Labeling and Education Act into law.

BUT THE FIGHT TO PROTECT CONSUMERS AGAINST MISLEADING health claims wasn't nearly over. Buried within the NLEA like a ticking time bomb was the deal we'd struck with Hatch to let the FDA decide how to regulate dietary supplements. The agency was given one year after President Bush signed the law to examine the issue and recommend a course of action. In what must have seemed an extraordinary stroke of luck to Hatch, his own former aide, David Kessler, became commis-sioner of the FDA on the same day the NLEA became law.

That made it all the more stunning when, in November 1991, Kessler released the agency's findings: Rather than the lighter regulations Hatch anticipated, the FDA announced that dietary supplements posed a serious health risk and ought to be regulated exactly like the NLEA regulated food. The FDA had already convened a task force on dietary supplements to study the dangers. We could scarcely have imagined a better outcome. But Kessler's findings sent supplement manufactur-ers into a tizzy, and the $4 billion-a-year industry quickly mobi-lized a wide-ranging campaign to fight back. To my surprise, I found myself in the crosshairs.

The industry devised a clever two-track strategy. The first part entailed having Hatch introduce a Senate bill, the Health Freedom Act of 1992, and New Mexico's Bill Richardson a coun-terpart in the House, to establish the lax oversight they desired. Both bills precluded FDA regulation of dietary supplements as drugs, denied the agency the power to approve them before they hit the market, and removed the NLEA's requirement that "significant scientific agreement" back up any health claims, giving manufacturers unfettered ability to assert whatever they wished about their products, including that supplements could cure cancer and AIDS. The second part of the strategy involved an enforcement bill I had recently introduced to strengthen the FDA's historically weak powers of oversight by granting it, for the first time, the ability to issue subpoenas, force the recall of dangerous products, and, if necessary, confiscate such products. The bill sought to shore up broad deficiencies and was not aimed at dietary supplements specifically—indeed, did not even mention them. But the supplement industry seized on it to make the claim that the government intended to outlaw most supplements and require prescriptions for the benign few, like vitamin C, that might still be allowed on store shelves. "Don't let them take our vitamins away!" became the industry's rallying cry.

This cynical portrayal had not the slightest basis in reality. But it was effective nonetheless. People who use dietary supplements tend to feel passionately about them, and by scaring these customers into believing that the government was going to take them away, the industry was able to mount an enormous grassroots lobbying effort. Every health food store in the country set up a booth with preaddressed postcards that outraged customers could send to their congressman. Some even had posters on the wall identifying me as the culprit trying to force them to get a doctor's prescription for their vitamins. But the highlight of the industry's campaign of scare tactics was a television commercial starring the actor Mel Gibson. In the ad, Gibson is seen wearing a bathrobe and standing in the kitchen of an enormous mansion late at night. He is about to take a vitamin when suddenly an army of machine-gun-wielding agents in black "FDA" jackets bursts into the house. "Guys—it's only vitamins!" Gibson cries helplessly, his hands raised in the air. The agents grab him anyway, and a message flashes across the screen: "Write Congress Now. Protect your right to use vitamins and other supplements."

The Gibson commercial, and the broader campaign of which it was a part, tapped into a strain of populist paranoia in the country that crosses every geographic and political boundary. This paranoia centers on the belief that a vast conspiracy is at work between doctors, drug companies, and the federal government to try and force people to use expensive pharmaceuticals, which might even make them sicker, while at the same time denying them access to "natural ingredients" like Chinese herbs that have been used for thousands of years to keep people healthy. It all boiled down to the belief that doctors and drug companies *needed* people to get sick in order to make money—and that any measure seeking to strengthen FDA enforcement powers was clear evidence of congressional complicity. The supplement industry made very clever use of these passionately misguided beliefs about "the system" and how it operated. By conflating two bills, it managed to create a phony threat (my enforcement bill) and at the same time rally its customers behind an industry-friendly "solution" (Hatch-Richardson) that stripped away even the most basic health and safety provisions.

As chairman of the health subcommittee, any supplement bill had to get past me before it could become law. The industry's initial foray in 1992, the Health Freedom Bill, arrived too late in the year to get through Congress. So Hatch tried to attach a rider to an appropriations bill that was sure to pass that established a one-year moratorium on applying NLEA standards to dietary supplements. Though his amendment passed the Senate by a 94-1 vote, we managed to kill it in the House-Senate conference. But we could not stop his next attempt, which he attached to a prescription drug bill in the closing weeks of Congress. Aware of the deep suspicion with which supplement users regarded the FDA, Hatch's amendment fanned the flames by directing the Department of Health and Human Services to produce a report on the FDA's enforcement practices, and determine whether the agency discriminated against dietary supplements. (The report would conclude it did not.)

The following year, Hatch and Richardson tried again. Their bills soon became the focus of public attention, aided by the uproar that greeted the June 1993 release of the task force on dietary supplements report, which concluded that some ingredients in popular supplements should indeed be regulated as drugs. A few weeks later, I held a subcommittee hearing in an attempt to bring some balance to the public debate by providing facts to counter the industry spin. I announced my hope of finding a legislative solution that would guarantee the availability of safe dietary supplements as long as they made no unproven claims. Testifying in support of this goal, Kessler reiterated that the FDA was "not concerned about [vitamins and minerals] as long as the potencies are reasonable, their health claims are scientifically valid, and they are manufactured under appropriate quality control standards." He reminded the committee of the significant health issues at stake, referencing the new FDA report that found "hundreds and hundreds of dietary supplements that claim to cure, treat or reduce the risk of a variety of health problems, some as serious as cancer and AIDS."

But all this was to little avail. Not long afterward, retailers organized a national blackout day on which stores draped their supplement shelves in black so consumers could "see" what products Congress intended to outlaw. A massive mail and telephone campaign swamped Capitol Hill. Supposedly, more people wrote to Congress about dietary supplements that year than about any other issue.

Throughout my career, I have regarded myself as the good guy fighting the special interests. But this time, the public outcry hit close to home, and I found myself cast in the unaccustomed role of villain. Los Angeles lives up to its health-conscious stereotype, and everywhere I went I seemed to encounter angry constituents. Letters poured into my office. Wives of Hollywood studio executives called me to complain. While visiting a synagogue, a man stood up and berated me for the bill. I vividly recall one community meeting at which a bodybuilder in a red tank top, veins bulging from his neck, screamed at me for what he mistakenly imagined was my crusade to deny him muscle-building supplements. Most people, without screaming about it, took the well-intentioned position that these were "natural products" that they should be able to use, not realizing the extent of the misinformation they'd absorbed.

THE FIGHT TO REGULATE DIETARY SUPPLEMENTS HELD MANY SIMIlarities to others in my legislative career: We found ourselves in the customary position of underdog, facing a larger, better-funded opponent with many powerful allies. This time, we did enjoy considerable media support, as most major newspapers editorialized against the Hatch-Richardson bills and did a good job of explaining the risks posed by many supplements. But the press was no match for the intensity of the opposition, and ultimately did not rally much support to our cause. People often believe the worst about public officials. And when voters are mad enough, those officials usually listen.

Early in 1994, efforts to reach a joint House-Senate compromise fell apart, as did a subsequent attempt between Hatch and Ted Kennedy, who chaired the Labor and Human Resources

Committee through which the Senate bill had to pass. In the end, the pressure was so great that the bill passed over Kennedy's objection.

The industry trade group worked to stoke a similar mutiny among supporters in the House, where I had steadfastly refused to call up the Richardson bill (even though more than half the House—261 members—had co-sponsored it). We tried heading them off by introducing our own bill, which aimed to counter the industry's most effective scare tactic by forbidding government from requiring prescriptions for vitamins. But lacking credibility with the other side, this gambit failed. Meanwhile, pressure to move Richardson's bill mounted to the point that our opponents began laying the groundwork for a discharge petition—a rarely invoked rule that allows a majority of House members (218 votes) to override a chairman and forcibly "discharge," or remove, a bill from committee and place it for consideration on the floor.

It was clear where the momentum was heading. My staff and I understood that a moment of reckoning was nearly at hand, and recognized further the grim irony of our predicament: Just as the prospect of near-certain defeat had forced industry groups to negotiate on NLEA, the fight over supplements that originated in the same legislation had now reached a similar point, only this time with the roles reversed. Rather than forfeit our last chance to make a bad law slightly better, we sat down to negotiate with Hatch, Kennedy, and Dingell.

Hatch's bill had passed the Senate, so it became the vehicle for our discussions. The debate initially centered on the issue of safety. Though the FDA would not be able to approve or regulate supplements, everyone agreed that if a safety issue were to arise, the agency needed to have the ability to act. Beyond that, we split. The endless contention over health claims remained the key point of difference: industry's desire to escape any limitations at all versus our refusal to accept unproven claims for curing disease. The negotiations eventually narrowed to the precise question of how the claims could be worded.

Finally, Hatch's side proposed that rather than direct claims to treat diseases or conditions ("Product X lowers blood pressure"), manufacturers be permitted to make more general ones regarding a product's purported effect on the body ("Product X will bolster your immune system"). This, too, concerned me. In 1994, practical measures to strengthen the immune system held great interest owing to the prevalence of AIDS (acquired immunodeficiency syndrome), and the suggestion that a dietary supplement lacking FDA approval might make any meaningful difference seemed sure to cause harm. I expressed my skepticism. They wouldn't budge. Then someone said, "What if we added a disclaimer stating that FDA had not validated the claim?"

For two brutal years, I had struggled with paltry support, and to little evident effect, in what everyone could now see was a losing fight. Dispirited and exhausted, I did something uncharacteristic: I agreed, right there at the table. From the looks on their faces, I could see that my staff was taken aback. The secret to successful negotiations is never answering right away. Over the years, we'd won numerous important concessions on all sorts of bills by following a disciplined routine when presented with these sorts of proposals. Experience taught me to ask for a recess, talk to the experts on my staff, and then offer a counterproposal, or, if necessary, simply decline. This careful approach provided a negotiating advantage over the many members who would "get ahead of their staff," as the phrase had it, and cut deals without pausing to consider the larger ramifications, as I had just done.

I could tell right away that my staff believed I had needlessly conceded an important fight. But as Dingell pointed out, I had agreed to the offer of an FDA disclaimer and now had to honor my word. This final barrier cleared, the bill moved rapidly through both chambers, and on October 25, 1994, President Bill Clinton signed the Dietary Supplement Health and Education Act into law.

DESPITE THE SETBACK WITH DIETARY SUPPLEMENTS, THE NUTRItion Labeling and Education Act of 1990 has functioned almost exactly as Congress intended. In a happy case of serendipity, Ed Madigan became secretary of agriculture shortly after the bill passed, and issued an order extending nutrition-labeling requirements to meat and poultry (which were not covered by the NLEA). Today, finding honest, accurate information about the foods we eat has never been easier, and the benefits to health-conscious consumers have been immeasurable.

From a public standpoint, too, the NLEA has been a success. Most media coverage of Washington focuses disproportionately on "big issues," like the president's budget, that often have little impact on the lives of most Americans (Congress generally ignores the president's budget and does as it pleases). Meanwhile, smaller issues like food labeling fly under the radar, but nonetheless have a revolutionary impact on most people's lives, even if they don't realize it. Whether strictly adhering to the South Beach Diet or simply trying to keep an eye on sodium or cholesterol intake, it's a good bet that most Americans make use of nutrition labels every day of their lives. In fact, knowing what you're eating has become so commonplace that it's hard to imagine there was ever a time when you *couldn't* get basic nutrition information on food labels.

The fact that the law has turned out to be so useful is especially gratifying, since it came about not because of public demand, but rather by congressional initiative. It's a good example of the leadership that critics so often claim is lacking in Washington. Much as Proposition 65's threat of a warning label prompted manufacturers to provide healthier food in California, today's nutrition labels function the same way on a national scale by empowering consumers who want to buy healthier foods and in turn forcing companies to supply them. We're a healthier country because Congress acted.

The only smirch on our original effort is the Dietary Supplement Health and Education Act of 1994. As a lesson in politics, DSHEA is instructive because it shows how industry can concoct an issue based entirely on misinformation that ultimately allows it to circumvent the law. Sometimes spin trumps fact. When the context is a political campaign, most people understand this and guard against it. But they're not nearly as used to being deceived in a legislative campaign. The industry's decision to use health food stores as the vehicle to accomplish this was especially effective since many people instinctively trust them to be an impartial source of information, much like their doctor, and in reality they were not. The vast majority of consumers never realized that the outcry against Congress was being financed by the supplement industry.

As policy, DSHEA has been every bit as harmful as we feared, demonstrating anew that any market lacking regulation or the need to ensure safety quickly sinks to the lowest common denominator. The FDA disclaimer doesn't seem to have had the slightest impact on how people use supplements. Since the law went into effect, a number of them have proved to have serious health effects. For years, the most popular over-the-counter weight loss supplement, an herbal stimulant called ephedra, was linked to heart attacks, strokes, and seizures. Only the death in 2003 of Baltimore Orioles pitcher Steve Bechler, who had been using ephedra, caused sufficient notoriety for the FDA to finally ban it. Many other dangerous substances are still for sale.

Since the legislative loss on dietary supplements, we have

continued to press for changes in the law and, along with getting ephedra off the market, have made slow but steady progress toward that end. After the September 11 attacks, when unscrupulous companies began marketing supplements as "cures" for anthrax and other bioterrorism agents, we were able to get a provision into the Bioterrorism Act of 2002 forbidding this practice and requiring all supplement companies to register with the FDA and track the source of their ingredients. In 2006, we passed a law requiring manufacturers to report adverse reactions, like those caused by ephedra, to the FDA. Other measures made it through Congress, only to be ignored by the Bush administration.

With a new administration in power, that, too, could soon change. In time, bad laws always reveal themselves. And one enduring truth about Washington is that no issue is ever settled for good.

CHAPTER 7

Pesticides and Food

ONE FREQUENT COMPLAINT ABOUT CONGRESS IS THAT partisan differences make it all but impossible to reach agreement on many of our most pressing problems. Some things, this line of thinking goes, are simply too divisive or controversial ever to be resolved. While the increased hostility between Democrats and Republicans certainly poses a hurdle, it is hardly insurmountable. The example of how the government came to regulate harmful pesticides that were making their way into the foods we eat illustrates how bipartisan cooperation can happen—and how sometimes, even on issues of tremendous importance, the public may not even realize that it has occurred. By the mid-1990s, the problem of what to do about pesticides had frustrated Congress for almost two decades, until members of my staff and the staff of Tom Bliley, a Virginia Republican, met secretly with representatives of a few key government agencies for three days of negotiations. This negotiating session solved a seemingly intractable problem by producing a new law to regulate pesticides that was both easier for industry to comply with and vastly improved health protections for millions of American families.

In 1995, a woman named Nancy Chuda came to my office to lobby me about the effects of pesticides on children. A few years earlier, Nancy's five-year-old daughter, Collette, had died of a rare, nongenetic kidney cancer called Wilms' Tumor that was generally believed to be caused by exposure to chemical pesticides. Nancy wanted Congress to pass stricter safety standards for pesticides, and she had solid evidence to justify why this was a good idea. A number of recent studies had established a link between environmental toxins like pesticides and childhood cancer. And at the time, environmental protection standards in the United States were based on determinations of the potential effects of carcinogens on a 155-pound adult male. Children are obviously much more vulnerable to dangerous chemicals than fully grown adults.

My subcommittee, Health and the Environment, had legislative and oversight jurisdiction over water, air, and food. Establishing appropriate safety standards to protect children, and especially infants, from pesticides was a goal that had long eluded me. The pesticide industry grew out of the chemical weapons industry of World War II. After the war, chemical companies discovered that many of the substances they produced were effective killers of weeds and bugs and could be put to use by America's farmers. Chloropicrin, a World War I chemical warfare agent thought to have DNA-damaging effects, became an effective fumigant to kill plant root fungi and bacteria (it is also an active ingredient in tear gas). Organophosphate pesticides were originally developed in Germany during the 1930s as nerve agents for military use. Little was done in the way of health and safety testing. These pesticides and others like them were routinely being used on fruits and vegetables.

Over the years, a gradual awareness of these health risks

had begun to take hold. In 1962, Rachel Carson's book *Silent Spring* alerted the public to the environmental dangers of DDT and similar agents. The environmental movement of the 1970s furthered this cause. In 1989, the Alar scare, prompted by a *60 Minutes* broadcast about the cancer-causing chemical that apple growers sprayed on their trees only for it to make its way into children's apple juice, led to heightened awareness of the dangers of pesticides on food. But none of this was enough to create the momentum necessary to pass meaningful safety standards. A Clinton administration bill offered in 1993 to limit the use of pesticides had gone nowhere.

One difficulty confronting major pesticide legislation was that, in contrast to similar health issues like safe drinking water and clean air, most people didn't have a clear concept of the problem and its effect. The clean air debate in the United States was transformed overnight in 1984 when methyl isocyanate gas leaked from the Union Carbide chemical plant in Bhopal, India, instantly killing more than three thousand people. Lacking such a vivid illustration of its dangers, the problem of pesticides had lingered unresolved for years, even though some of the products sprayed on crops derived from the very same chemical, methyl isocyanate, that had laid Bhopal to waste. In part for these reasons, pesticides also didn't rate as high a priority for the major environmental groups, so outside support was hard to come by as well.

In oversight hearings, the subcommittee had nevertheless made every attempt to convey the horror of how cancers had destroyed children like Collette Chuda and to highlight reports like the landmark 1993 study by the National Academy of Sciences that connected the alarmingly frequent instances of childhood cancer with pesticides. So the issue could be dramatized—but our efforts to do so usually produced only one-day stories. Good legislation is the fruit of a complicated process that requires sustained pressure and attention. The problem with generating public interest about pesticides was that it was hard to pinpoint the effects, however deadly, on particular people. The gap between a period of prolonged exposure and the onset of disease—as contrasted with the sudden deaths by asphyxiation in Bhopal—also made it easier for our opponents to block our efforts. The chemical companies would besiege members of Congress with elaborate charts and numbers to "prove" that legislation like the Clinton bill that sought to curtail the use of chemical pesticides would without a doubt bankrupt the industry.

Another obstacle stemmed from a quirk of the law: It placed completely different regulations on raw foods and processed foods, particularly for cancer-causing substances. This had the perverse effect of imposing very strong standards on processed foods and very weak standards on raw foods, an anomaly that had kept industry and public interest groups at war for almost forty years. The main source of contention was an obscure legal provision known as the Delaney Clause. The Delaney Clause was a 1958 measure named after Representative James Delaney of New York that banned from processed foods "any chemical additive known to induce cancer." The capacity to measure the amount of carcinogens in food was not very sophisticated in 1958. But by the 1970s, the technology had advanced to the point where even trace amounts could be detected. This created a headache for farmers and food manufacturers. Many of the pesticides they had relied on for years were now showing up as carcinogens in processed foods, putting manufacturers in technical violation of the Delaney Clause. The industry dealt with this problem in two ways. Beginning in the late 1970s, its allies in Congress urged that the clause be weakened or preempted. At the same time, it pressured state and federal regulators not to enforce the law too strictly, lest it drive them out of business. For a long while, this approach seemed to work. The Delaney Clause was a strong law on the books, but it simply was not being enforced. Finally, public interest groups that supported the strict standard sued for tougher enforcement, and in 1992 the Ninth Circuit Court of Appeals in San Francisco ruled that the government must uphold the absolute ban on carcinogens.

But the Delaney Clause did not apply to raw foods, and the laws that did apply were awful—in effect, permitting farmers to use chemical weapons to treat their crops. This was especially harmful to children, who tend to eat more fresh fruits and vegetables than adults do. Everyone knew the law didn't work because it didn't cover raw foods the way it should have. And yet it seemed impossible to fix. In exchange for not blocking stronger raw food laws, industry demanded the repeal of the Delaney Clause, which would weaken the regulation of processed foods.

IN 1994, THE POLITICS OF PESTICIDES, AND EVERYTHING ELSE, WAS upended when Republicans won control of the House of Representatives, changing the culture of Congress overnight. Re publican issues suddenly took precedence, which meant that industries' interests often trumped the broader public good. Republicans not only controlled the committees, but also the rules. One of their first acts was to repeal many of the parliamentary maneuvers I had used in the past to delay legislation, like Reagan's Clean Air Act amendments, that seemed dangerous. Most significantly, Republicans completely overturned the committee system that had obtained since long before my arrival in Congress. The old system, in which chairmen like Paul Rogers took careful account of everyone's views, and members of both parties deferred to the expertise of committees and subcommittees, gave way to a rigid hierarchy in which the only view that mattered was the view of the new Republican leadership.

What had been a "bottom-up" process now became "top-down" in a way that distinctly recalled how the California Assembly had operated under Jesse Unruh. All decisions flowed from the top. Ideologues like Newt Gingrich and Tom DeLay, who dominated the Republican leadership, had little interest in anyone else's input, including those members of their own party who didn't fall into line. Republican chairmen quickly realized that they served at the pleasure of their leadership, and that the leadership's only concern was ramming through the provisions of the "Contract With America," a list of right-wing grievances that had featured prominently in the 1994 midterm elections. Rather than draft bills, these chairmen were handed legislation by the leadership (often written by lobbyists) and ordered to pass it in a matter of days. Sometimes there would be a hearing; other times there wouldn't be. Debate was curtailed, amendments often limited or forbidden, and on many occasions members weren't even given enough time to read the bills they were being asked to vote on. As a result, many members (especially Democrats, who were shut out of the drafting process) didn't have much of an understanding of the legislation passed through Congress during this period. Congress had stopped functioning as a legislative body wherein committees with relevant expertise wrote the nation's laws, but instead became a rubber stamp for the most powerful elements of the Republican Party. And "consensus" became a bad word.

It wasn't long before the Republican leadership turned to the issue of pesticides—or rather, to satisfying the food industry's desire to at last repeal the Delaney Clause. The instrument for doing so was a bill sponsored by Tom Bliley, the Virginia Republican and chairman of the House Energy and Commerce Committee, that appeared to have been written by industry lobbyists. You can usually determine a bill's provenance by checking certain markings on it. When a congressman's staff writes a bill, the formal text is prepared by the House Office of Legislative Counsel, which ensures that existing statutes are properly amended and the new measure's language conforms to the necessary rules. When a bill has undergone this process, each page carries an HLC file number. What gave the Republican pesticide draft away (apart from its content, an industry wish list) was its lack of HLC markings—an absence true of much of what the new Republican leadership introduced. Needless to say, the prospects for my own bill, mandating disclosure of carcinogens in all foods and setting safety standards for kids, did not look very rosy.

Because the Appeals Court had ruled that the Delaney Clause must be enforced, Republicans were rather urgently set on repealing or preempting it. By the summer of 1996, we were very much on the defensive and stood a good chance of getting rolled. But powerful as it was, Bliley's contingent faced an unwelcome reality: Even if the bill got through Congress, President Clinton would almost surely veto it. Were that to happen, the food industry would have to contend with the full weight of the Delaney Clause.

House Republicans had an additional worry. For all their *Sturm und Drang*, few provisions of the "Contract With America" had actually made their way into law. And their leadership had committed a serious tactical error when it shut down the federal government during a November 1995 budget dispute with the White House, a maneuver that backfired when the public blamed the Republicans, rather than Bill Clinton, for the fiasco. With the 1996 election looming, House Republicans were beginning to realize that they had precious little to show voters in the way of tangible accomplishments.

These conditions created a perfect opportunity for bipartisan compromise. Although Bliley and I hailed from opposite ends of the political spectrum and our views diverged on almost every issue, we had developed a good relationship. Bliley, a mortician by trade and a serious Catholic, hailed from Richmond, Virginia. His manner was always gentlemanly and proper. I had come to know him over the years and regarded him with fondness and respect. Once, on a congressional delegation to Prague, Bliley and his wife had joined Janet and me for Passover Seder. This friendliness eventually led us to collaborate on legislation. Only a month or so before the pesticide issue came to a head, we had put aside our strong policy disagreements and struck a deal to renew the Safe Drinking Water Act. Recognizing that it would be nearly impossible to pass my own pesticide bill, but also that Republicans were growing desperate for an achievement, I sensed that even in the minority we might be able to insist on something strong. So I suggested to Bliley that it might be worthwhile to get together in secret and conduct a hypothetical negotiation to see if we could reach an agreement on pesticides.

Bliley instantly recognized the attraction of this unusual approach. Secrecy afforded us the cover to move away from long-held positions that would have generated an outcry from interest groups on both sides were it conducted in public—one of the great recurrent problems of trying to hash out a bipartisan bill. We agreed that our staffs would sit down for three days to work out a comprehensive deal, both of us vowing to honor the terms if they emerged successful. If they failed, no one else would know that Henry Waxman had been willing to preempt the Delaney Clause or that Tom Bliley had entertained the notion of tougher safety standards on raw foods. No one wants to be caught making major concessions until they're certain a deal can be struck. Here, the ground rules assured we wouldn't have to.

There remained an element of risk to both sides. In any such negotiation, political considerations bump up against policy goals. My agreeing to a deal would hand Republicans an accomplishment they could cite while campaigning against Democrats in the upcoming election. But it would also strengthen a law that we had been fighting to improve for nearly two decades, and the effect would be to protect children and adults from dangerous pesticides, which would ultimately save lives. A perennial dilemma for any congressman is whether to trade bad politics for good policy. Doing so on pesticides struck me as well worthwhile.

We began one Wednesday morning in July. Assembled along with my chief of staff, and Bliley's, were representatives of the committee's ranking member, John Dingell, the FDA, and EPA, as well as the food industry and environmental organizations. One group absent from the proceedings was lobbyists. A common misconception about Washington is that lobbyists pull the strings. But most of them are former committee staffers whose job is merely to monitor developments and report back to the industry officials who employ them. Negotiating with lobbyists is a tedious and time-consuming affair because they are not usually empowered to make decisions and first must check with their clients, who in turn must check with their lawyers before a decision can be made. Lawyers are the only ones on the industry side steeped in the gritty details. Phil Schiliro, my chief of staff, wisely insisted that everyone involved here be given the power to make decisions.

Once underway, talks proceeded quickly. Our side wanted stronger standards for raw foods, and was willing to give a little on processed foods in order to get them; the food industry wanted to get out from under the Delaney Clause, badly enough that it was willing to yield on raw foods. While the liberal public interest groups were adamant about upholding Delaney, I was prepared to consider a law that stopped short of an outright ban on carcinogens. While I was perfectly content to live with the Delaney Clause, the truth is that so strict a standard was actually tougher than it needed to be, since trace amounts of many harmful substances are often benign. By Friday night, we had settled on the broad but rigorous standard that any pesticides used on foods must carry a "reasonable certainty of no harm" and take special account of vulnerable populations like infants and children. "Reasonable certainty" was defined as a one-in-a-million chance of causing cancer. The food industry was liberated from Delaney and avoided having to take a number of pesticides off the market.

On Saturday, the House Legislative Counsel drafted the agreement. The following week, it sailed through subcommittee and committee, and then won the unanimous approval of the House. A week later, the Senate passed the bill verbatim, and it was off to the president's desk. It was not a tough sell. When Phil called to inform Clinton's chief of staff, Leon Panetta, that we had reached a compromise on pesticides and started explaining the particulars, Panetta stopped him. "If Waxman and Bliley are together on this," he said, "I don't need to know anymore. We're for it."

THE RESOLUTION OF THE PESTICIDE ISSUE AFTER ALMOST TWO DEcades of frustrated stalemate happened so suddenly, and so quietly, that the scope of the achievement almost didn't register. The news media are conditioned to assume that the most important political issues are the ones that create the greatest amount of public drama and culminate in gavel-pounding showdowns on the House floor. They didn't quite know how to treat the announcement of our deal, so the response was muted. Even some sophisticated participants didn't fully grasp what to make of it. When I called Nancy Chuda with word that we had accomplished our goal, the news was so unexpected that at first it seemed not to register. This set me to pondering the old line about a tree falling in the forest: When a law of real weight is enacted without anyone noticing, does it still count as an accomplishment?

But, of course, the important thing was not public fanfare but the quality of the new law. We had managed to pass a uniform national pesticide standard that would protect the health and safety of all Americans—and we had done so from a position of considerable weakness. Three things made this possible. The first was my relationship with Tom Bliley. Despite party differences, we implicitly trusted one another not to go public, had things not worked out, with the details of what the other had been willing to concede. Second was the fact that all those at the table were empowered to make decisions. And third, they were fully prepared to see them through. The only way this type of negotiation can succeed is to tackle the whole problem in one fell swoop, so that news of the deal arrives concurrently with the endorsements of all the major interests. Aside from a handful of staunch advocates of the Delaney Clause who criticized me, the new law—formally the Food Quality Protection Act of 1996—came off without a hitch.

ONE OF THE LAW'S CRITICAL ACHIEVEMENTS WAS THAT IT ESTAB-lished an underlying principle for how pesticides would be regulated that favored public health over industry interests. Since the 1950s, food manufacturers had argued that laws regulating pesticide use should be driven by the cost of compliance—it was, that is to say, desirable to protect the public health only insofar as the cost of doing so did not weigh too heavily on farmers and food processors. The public interest community countered this notion with the assertion that the goal of any pesticide law should, first and foremost, be to protect the public health. The Food Quality Protection Act was a triumph in part because the requirement that any pesticide used must carry a "reasonable certainty of no harm" was a "health-based," rather than a "cost-based," standard: No matter what it cost industry, pesticides that exacted a serious effect on health were blocked from human consumption.

This is exactly how the law operated—and what happened next should serve as a reminder that even the best-written laws have unintended consequences, and as such must constantly be updated and strengthened to ensure that they are performing the function Congress intended.

Under the new law, the EPA took responsibility for regulating pesticides according to the health-based standard, the hope being that this would diminish health risks and encourage farmers to use safer pesticides. But as this began happening, the manufacturers of the more dangerous chemical pesticides realized that they would have to stop making them unless they could somehow find a way to meet the new safety standard.

Measuring the health effects of pesticides necessarily entails a measure of informed guesswork. At the time of the Food Quality Protection Act, the process involved giving animals strong doses over a short period of time, seeing what happened to them, and extrapolating the likely effects on human beings. If a large dose of something appears to be safe in animals—if it didn't correlate with cancers or reproductive or developmental problems—chances are that a much smaller dose is not likely to harm humans. Scientists use this information to develop risk models for the effects of individual pesticides, and can pluck food right off supermarket shelves and test it to see if it complies. They have even developed a rule of thumb for what constitutes a safe level for human ingestion, which they call the Two Tenfold Safety Factor. Once a safe threshold among animals has been determined, they will reduce that amount tenfold (an appropriate level of caution for human exposure) and then do so once more (since some people are going to be more sensitive than others). Hence, the Two Tenfold Safety Factor. Because the new law required stricter standards for infants and children, yet a third tenfold safety factor was included to make the standard even stronger. The increase from two to three tenfolds was enough to render some pesticides unusable on foods. So the chemical industry, seeing that mathematics lay at the heart of their problem, realized that it could challenge the formula—and remove one tenfold safety factor—if, instead of testing pesticides on animals, it was allowed to test them directly on human beings.

The Clinton administration refused to permit this and imposed a moratorium on human testing. But when George W. Bush became president, he ushered in an era of unfettered deregulation that rivaled even the Reagan era. Sensing correctly that the tide had changed, the chemical industry set out once more to persuade regulators to accept human testing. In October 2001, the EPA's assistant administrator, Stephen L. Johnson, announced at a meeting of the American Crop Protection Association, the pesticide industry trade group, that the Bush administration would indeed give human testing the green light. To her credit, Christie Todd Whitman, Bush's first EPA administrator, refused to go along with this. But Whitman soon found herself unwelcome in the administration, and left in 2003. By the time Johnson took over the EPA in 2005, he had already put his own views on human testing into practice.

One of the most appalling programs that Johnson initiated was the Children's Environmental Exposure Research Study (known by the bizarre acronym CHEERS). The study, which was partially financed by the chemical industry, sought to examine the effects of pesticides on low-income children, whose families—furnished with $970, a video camera, and CHEERS

T-shirts and baby bibs—were asked to record the chemical exposure for two years, during which EPA scientists would periodically collect urine samples.

The CHEERS program was halted only after coming to light during Johnson's confirmation hearings, and even then only grudgingly. But the Bush EPA continued to allow the human testing of pesticides. Alarmed by this trend, I joined with Senator Barbara Boxer of California to commission a report establishing just what tests were being undertaken, whom they were being undertaken on, and whether they had any scientific merit.

The report uncovered "significant and widespread deficiencies" in the two dozen human pesticide experiments that had been considered, or were in the process of being considered, by the EPA, some of them decades old and many of them conducted overseas (oddly enough, Scotland seems to be a haven for human testing). "In violation of ethical standards," the report stated, "the experiments appear to have inflicted harm on human subjects, dismissed adverse outcomes, and lacked scientific validity." Among the tests were cases where subjects had been dosed with organophosphates (used as nerve agents by the German army) and methyl isocyanate (the Bhopal gas); others had been placed in a gas chamber with chloropicrin (the active ingredient in tear gas)—and in doses well beyond federal exposure limits; in several experiments, the subjects were instructed to take pills of insecticide with their breakfast orange juice.

The adverse effects that these tests documented were routinely dismissed. A twenty-eight-day test of azinphos-methyl, a pesticide produced by the Bayer Corporation, on eight subjects produced headaches, abdominal pain, nausea, coughing, and rashes. The researchers concluded that every adverse reaction was unrelated to the chemical being tested, instead attributing most of them to "viral illness." A six-month study of dichlorvos, a pesticide manufactured by American Vanguard, included youngsters from two to nineteen, whose homes were outfitted with resin strips containing dichlorvos. When a teenage girl complained of headaches, the researchers removed the resin strip from her bedroom and the headaches stopped. Yet they still concluded that this, too, was not caused by the pesticide: "Questioning of the parent revealed the likelihood that the headaches were produced by other pressures."

Scientifically valid drug tests ordinarily require thousands of human clinical trials to determine safety and efficacy, and even then often miss particular effects. Many of the human pesticide experiments involved no more than a handful of subjects. One study had but a single subject: The researcher dosed himself. Yet the Bush administration justified this combination of the dangerous with the arbitrary by arguing that such studies were "available, relevant, and appropriate."

Congress responded to the news that human beings—including children—were being used as lab rats by attaching a rider to an appropriations bill that prohibited the EPA from "accepting, considering, or relying upon" these types of studies until strict procedural standards had been established. While the amendment did garner the support of many religious conservatives who were troubled by the moral and ethical implications of intentionally dosing people with toxic chemicals, many Republicans still lined up behind the pesticide industry. But rather than engage in a public fight on an issue where the politics so clearly did not favor them, they let the bill pass, and President Bush eventually signed it into law.

In February 2006, the EPA issued a new rule on human testing that imposed some restrictions but stopped short of banning it outright. (Johnson still wanted to keep the door open.) These new regulations established a Human Subjects Review

Board within EPA and forbade the agency to consider experiments on humans "intended for submission to EPA's pesticide program." Here is yet another example of how a single word can determine a law's effectiveness: When only those experiments "intended" for submission to the EPA are forbidden, a loophole opens for any other kind of human testing. So an industry group intent on getting around one tenfold safety factor could simply sponsor a test for "research" rather than regulatory purposes, and rest confident that the EPA would likely accept the study.

And this, of course, is exactly what happened. Though the Human Subjects Review Board has disallowed some human studies, it has let others be considered, thus weakening our protection against pesticides. The Natural Resources Defense Council has sued in federal court to overturn the EPA rule. Regardless of the outcome, this is an area that continues to demand vigorous congressional oversight.

But despite these ongoing skirmishes, the Food Quality Protection Act of 1996 has enjoyed a high degree of real success, with the public being exposed to fewer dangerous chemicals. It serves as a clear example of how Congress works to protect people even when the news media aren't paying careful attention. I can't help but find it somewhat ironic that since the 1990s, when we passed the Safe Drinking Water Act and the Food Quality Protection Act, there has been a huge shift in consumer behavior toward buying bottled spring water and organic foods. People obviously care a great deal about what sorts of chemicals they and their families consume, and they don't trust food makers to do a good enough job of regulating safety. The good news is that they no longer have to. Thanks to Congress, the worst pesticides are no longer used on foods.

The Art
of
Oversight

CHAPTER 8

Fraud, Waste, and Abuse

WHEN CIVICS TEXTBOOKS DESCRIBE CONGRESS, THEY tend to focus on the legislative process. But the congressional power of oversight is an equally important part of effective government. The Constitution invests Congress with the responsibility of overseeing the executive branch, a critical part of our nation's system of checks and balances. Proper oversight complements and strengthens the legislative process by identifying problems that may require new laws and by ensuring that existing laws are being executed as Congress meant them to be.

But the most basic oversight may also be the most important: simply ensuring that taxpayer money isn't squandered. Nothing inhibits effective government quite like fraud, waste, and abuse; and nothing breeds cynicism faster. One major reason public confidence in government has ebbed so dramatically since I arrived in Washington in 1975 is that we are too often confronted by abuses of the public trust: the $600 Pentagon toilet seat, for instance, or Alaska's "Bridge to Nowhere." Effective oversight identifies such outrageous examples of government waste and holds those responsible to account.

Government has the capacity to be a unique and extraordinary force for good. But regardless of ideology or partisan proclivity, every American should support the pursuit of fraud, waste, and abuse since a well-functioning Washington benefits everyone—and besides, our tax dollars are paying for it. Congress has a crucial responsibility to make government as effective and efficient as possible and to make sure that the people's money isn't wasted, whether through incompetence or deceit. To this end, it's vitally important that every facet of government be subjected to potential scrutiny.

The hub of this scrutiny in the House of Representatives is the Committee on Oversight and Government Reform, which is responsible for ensuring that federal laws and programs are being carried out as Congress intended. Its members help determine whether government programs should be continued, curtailed, or eliminated. Congress assigns each committee oversight jurisdiction over its particular area of competence—the Financial Services Committee covers banking, the Veterans' Affairs Committee covers health care and benefits for military veterans, and so on. But Oversight is unique in that House rules give it nearly unlimited power to investigate any matter, regardless of whether another committee has concurrent jurisdiction. Its chairman is therefore entrusted with enormous power and latitude—and an accompanying obligation to use it responsibly.

I sat on the Oversight Committee for more than thirty years, as chairman from 2007 to 2008. Though oversight doesn't get nearly the popular attention of major acts of legislation, I consider many of my accomplishments in this area to be every bit as significant as the laws I've worked on. Though legislation and oversight are often thought of as distinct processes, they are in fact very much conjoined. For example, absent the years of oversight hearings on pollution, Bhopal, and acid rain, the Clean Air Act might never have come into being. Effective oversight can also negate the need for legislation: Simply bringing cases of fraud, waste, and abuse to light can quickly bring them to an end.

In recent years, the Oversight Committee has managed to identify and address all sorts of major problems: private contractors like Halliburton and its former subsidiary KBR overcharging the U.S. government in Iraq; insurers fleecing the Medicare prescription drug program, and others exploiting federal crop insurance for billions of dollars; government and private contractors who endangered the lives of Hurricane Katrina victims in New Orleans while still squandering hundreds of millions of dollars; boondoggle defense contracts worth billions more that bought Marine expeditionary fighting vehicles that don't run and deep-sea Coast Guard vessels that don't float. Through these investigations and many more, the Oversight Committee has held government to account and saved taxpayers billions of dollars.

But as with so much else in government, the committee's effectiveness has waxed and waned, depending on who controlled it and how they chose to use its powers. In fact, during my career, the Oversight Committee itself has shown how government can be a tremendous force for good—and how, when in the wrong hands, it can be an altogether different and harmful force.

AS A FRESHMAN CONGRESSMAN, I WAS ASSIGNED TO THE ENERGY and Commerce and the Science and Technology committees. Given my interest in health and environmental issues, Energy and Commerce was a perfect fit. But although Science and Technology did important work, I jumped at the chance to switch when a spot opened up on Oversight (then known as the Government Operations Committee) after my first term.

In 1977, Government Operations attracted some of the most active members of Congress, many of whom, like John Moss, were skilled subcommittee chairmen and masters of the art of oversight. Seeing them operate taught me a great deal that I later put to use as a chairman. And over the years, the committee performed a great deal of admirable work, investigating the progress of the war on cancer; pushing to open up government through the Freedom of Information Act; and bringing about procurement reform so that government (and thus taxpayers) pays less for goods and services. At President Carter's behest, we also did much to help create two new federal departments, Energy and Education.

But when the Republicans took over the House in 1995, the focus shifted away from strengthening government performance. House Republicans were consumed with bringing down President Clinton and viewed the powers of the Oversight Committee—in particular, the power to issue subpoenas—as valuable tools to that end. In fact, the Republican leadership considered Oversight so valuable and promising that they allotted it the largest budget of any committee in Congress.

In 1997, Cardiss Collins of Illinois retired, making me the committee's ranking minority member. At the same time, Dan Burton of Indiana took over as chairman. While I briefly held the hope that we might work together in a bipartisan fashion—I was no Clinton apologist and believed in strong oversight—that idea vanished quickly. Burton's zeal to pursue any allegation against Clinton, no matter how trivial or far-fetched, transformed the committee into a modern-day Star Chamber. (Before becoming chairman, Burton led a famous inquiry into the 1993 suicide of Vincent Foster, Clinton's deputy White House counsel; convinced Foster was murdered,

Burton re-created the event by shooting a pumpkin with a pistol in his backyard in an attempt to "prove" his theory.)

Burton and the Republican leadership wasted no time in getting down to business. One rule about government oversight that had applied since Senator Joseph McCarthy's Red Scare was that the chairman had to gain the consent of the ranking member before issuing a subpoena. If they disagreed, the committee would convene and vote on the matter. The majority party usually prevailed, but the process allowed for the minority to air its position before any decision went forward. The reason this rule had stood for so long is that subpoenaing a witness is a serious matter: The full force of the United States government demands that a citizen appear and reveal private information. Unlike a civil subpoena, a congressional subpoena cannot be challenged in court. When Burton took over in 1997, he overturned this long-standing precedent and gave himself unilateral power to summon witnesses and disclose information.

And he immediately proceeded to abuse it. Burton became notorious for fishing expeditions, usually in pursuit of Clinton, in which he would subpoena witnesses left and right, cavalierly reveal embarrassingly personal details, and issue outrageous accusations that would garner newspaper headlines across the country, but could rarely be substantiated.

Among his passions was trying to prove that Clinton was systematically selling out the country to China. One of his first truly appalling abuses came when he subpoenaed the financial and telephone records of a sixty-five-year-old Georgetown University professor named Chi Wang, whom his staff suspected of being involved in an improbable scheme to sell national security secrets to China in exchange for campaign contributions. But it turned out that they mistook Professor Wang for someone with a similar name. When I pointed this out, Burton's chief investigator admitted as much—but then proceeded to imply that Wang might nevertheless be guilty of *something*: "Whether he deserves a subpoena or not, we haven't decided." Here was an unmistakable example of unchecked and abusive government power. And rather than apologize, Burton's staff covered their retreat by casting aspersions on an innocent man.

Such callous recklessness became typical. It was Burton who subpoenaed young Elian González to prevent him from being returned to his father in Cuba. Even after Burton stepped down, the Republican leadership continued to misuse the Oversight Committee, as in 2005 when they subpoenaed Terri Schiavo—a young woman left in a persistent vegetative state by cardiac arrest—to appear before the committee in order to prevent her husband from removing her from life support.

Burton forced the Clinton administration to turn over millions of pages of documents and required high-ranking White House officials to be cross-examined by committee staff in depositions—but even so, he constantly complained of being stonewalled. At one point, to dramatize this claim for the television cameras, he had his staff erect an enormous "stone" wall (papier-mâché, actually) against one whole side of a hearing room, and then hung pictures of various people whom he alleged to be stonewalling. The hearing didn't generate a great deal of attention. But this arts-and-crafts project ruined the real wall, which had to be torn down and replaced at taxpayer expense. And we were the committee supposed to police government waste!

The turning point in the public's perception of Burton came when he released transcripts of prison recordings of the private telephone conversations of Webster Hubbell, the associate attorney general and old friend of the Clintons' who had been convicted for fraudulently billing his Arkansas law firm. Burton went on *Nightline* and *Meet the Press* to declare that the tapes implicated Hillary Clinton in the fraud. But my staff had carefully reviewed the same tapes and demonstrated that Burton or his staff had doctored the transcripts to omit key exonerating passages.

After the Hubbell fiasco, the press stopped responding to most of Burton's wilder allegations, and his hearings no longer made the front page. But by that time he had inflicted widespread damage. Along with exacting an incredible financial and psychological toll on the many innocent people he subpoenaed, Burton's actions ran up a steep, and entirely unjustified, bill for the U.S. taxpayers. The committee's minority staff calculated that from 1997 to 2002, the years of his chairmanship, Burton issued 1,052 unilateral subpoenas, most to probe alleged misconduct by the Clinton administration and the Democratic Party, at a total cost of more than $35 million.

Regrettably, there are few internal or external checks on such willful abuses. The Republicans held power and wielded it in whatever way they saw fit—not only on Oversight, but on nearly every other committee as well. This amounted to a broad-scale abuse of the public trust. One of the hardest things in government, especially for a committee chairman, is to exercise judiciousness and restraint. Employing the full powers invested in that position is often necessary and appropriate. But our system has few restraints, and Burton's lack of regard for rules and tradition undermined even these few. As Lord Acton famously declared, "Absolute power corrupts absolutely."

AS BAD AS THINGS WERE ON OVERSIGHT DURING THE CLINTON years, they got much worse when George W. Bush became president. Suddenly, the Republicans lost all interest in holding the executive branch to account. Their approach toward oversight changed entirely. When it concerned Bill Clinton, nothing was too small to investigate; but if it involved George W. Bush, it seemed as if nothing was so big that it couldn't be ignored—even if doing so had global consequences.

During the Burton years, the committee devoted more than 140 hours to hearings and depositions on whether President Clinton had misused his Christmas card list for political gain. But Republicans devoted fewer than ten hours to investigating reports that U.S. soldiers had tortured prisoners at Iraq's Abu Ghraib prison. Nor would they investigate the White House's role in misleading the public about Iraq's weapons of mass destruction, the original rationale for the invasion.

This absence of oversight encouraged a belief that no one would be held accountable for mistakes or even explicit misconduct, and fostered a culture in which officials throughout the Bush administration felt free to act with impunity. Congressional Republicans resisted overseeing the Republican White House, even as unequivocal failures began to mount. The tragedy of approaching oversight this way was that it neglected the committee's true purpose: Republicans paid too little attention to serious government failures that would have benefited from scrutiny and oversight, and instead devoted their efforts to investigating things like Martha Stewart's insider trading in pharmaceutical stocks.

From the minority, my staff and I tried to make up for this willful avoidance of responsibility. We did this primarily by writing letters. Lots of letters. As the committee's ranking member, I couldn't hold a hearing. But I could request records and information from the White House or from government agencies, and draw attention to whatever issue we were examining by releasing the letter to the media, which often picked up the story. This became a useful strategy, deployed so often that *The Washington Post* dubbed me "The Man of Letters."

Oftentimes we'd be stiffed, never receiving a reply. But

sometimes agencies would come through. And on very rare occasions, even the Bush White House would respond. For instance, just after the Enron scandal broke, I wrote to Vice President Dick Cheney requesting information about meetings the vice president had held with Enron's CEO, Ken Lay. Lay was well known as a big Republican donor and a close friend of the president's, so no Republican chairman had dreamed of holding a hearing. It looked as if Congress was going to ignore what was then the biggest bankruptcy in U.S. history. That is, until Cheney's office responded to my letter—and revealed that the vice president had met with Lay far more often than the public was aware. This opened a new line of inquiry that set the media in frantic pursuit.

At the same time, I formed a Special Investigations Division within the minority staff that interviewed whistle-blowers, pored over obscure government databases, and sometimes even went undercover. Because we were among the few people in Congress looking into Enron, whistle-blowers started coming forward. Taking a page from Attorney General John Ashcroft, who established a toll-free tip line to report suspicious behavior in the wake of the September 11 attacks, we established an Enron tip line and spread the word. This generated valuable new information, including nine videotapes of Ken Lay, the most damning of which captured him at a companywide meeting urging his employees to buy more Enron stock, even as he was frantically unloading his own holdings in anticipation of a share price collapse.

The Special Investigations Division eventually documented Enron's influence on the White House energy plan. It also released reports on the politicization of federal science and the growth of government secrecy. For one investigation, it purchased the curricula being used by federally funded abstinence-only programs and demonstrated that the Bush administration was spending hundreds of millions of dollars to mislead teens about the basic facts of reproductive health.

Beginning in 2003, the Oversight Committee experienced a marked improvement when Tom Davis, a moderate Republican from northern Virginia, took over. Unlike Burton, Davis recognized the value of responsible oversight and tried, within the strictures imposed by the Republican leadership, to reassert Congress's role. After the lobbyist Jack Abramoff was reported to have bilked Native American tribes and other clients out of millions of dollars, Davis agreed that the committee should act, and we jointly commenced an investigation into Abramoff's contacts with the White House. Davis also agreed to hearings on Halliburton's abuses in Iraq. In both cases, he became a partner in demanding information and pursuing the facts. But there were always limits on what we could do together. Though we were allowed to ask Abramoff's law firm to document his contacts with the White House, Davis would not consent to demand that the White House release its own records. And though we requested Defense Department audits of Halliburton's overbilling, we could not request documents that might have shed light on the role of Vice President Cheney, once head of the company.

Nevertheless, these joint endeavors were highly productive. The purpose of such hearings is not just to hold people to account and shine a spotlight on those who have abused the public trust, although these are important functions. Our goal is also to learn why and how the government malfunctions when it does, and what can be done to fix the problem. Often, patterns emerge that shed light on a given failure. A clear pattern in our investigations of the Bush administration was the government's growing use of private contractors to perform and even manage jobs that were once the direct responsibility of government. During Davis's tenure, and then during my own, one of Oversight's primary targets of inquiry thus became the vast and sudden increase of private contracting and the myriad ways—like "no-bid" and "cost-plus" contracts—in which these contractors squander taxpayer money.

My concern originated early in the Iraq War, when Halliburton was granted an enormous no-bid contract. Halliburton had a record of overcharging the government when it contracted to build barracks and feed U.S. troops in Yugoslavia. On closer inspection, this practice proved widespread. Not only were company officials marking up the price of everything from laundry ($100 a bag) to Coca-Cola ($35 a case); their employees were staying at five-star Kuwaiti hotels while U.S. troops slept in tents. But the full extent of the waste only became apparent after we dug deeper. Private companies like Halliburton often subcontract to smaller firms, which in turn subcontract to others, charging a fee at each step along the way, usually a percentage of the overall cost. So as a job worked its way down through multiple subcontractors, each added his fee to the bottom line. This is known as "cost-plus" contracting. One Halliburton official told us that the company mantra was "Don't worry about price. It's 'cost-plus.'" One needn't be a math whiz to understand how quickly this system inflates costs and even gives contractors an incentive to run up enormous bills.

The government compounded this problem by handing out no-bid contracts. The main argument conservatives make for wanting to outsource government work to the private sector is that the discipline of the free market will drive down the cost to taxpayers. But rather than have companies compete to provide the best price, the government did precisely the opposite, dividing Iraq into fiefdoms and dispensing no-bid contracts by geographic region. Halliburton got a contract for all the oil-related work in the south, Parsons in the north; Washington Group International did all electricity-related work in the north, while Perini Corporation got everything in the south. Had officials set out to design the *least* efficient way to rebuild Iraq they could hardly have topped this approach. It was analogous to hiring a different contractor to fix every room in your home and telling them, "Just fix what you think you need to and charge me 10 percent more than whatever it costs you—and feel free to pass the work on to whomever you like. Don't worry about the cost." Chances are you'd find yourself paying top dollar for poor service.

The reliance on private contractors was not limited to Iraq, nor was the no-bid, cost-plus approach. The same thing was rampant in the clean-up of Hurricane Katrina. Contractors would hire subcontractors, who would end up hiring a guy with a pickup truck to remove debris. Everyone added their fee, so everyone profited—except taxpayers, who were left with a $100 tab for a $10 job.

Why was this being allowed to happen? And why didn't the government clamp down? My investigators eventually discovered the answer. The job of oversight and management itself had also been handed over to private contractors, so there was no longer even a core of federal workers to monitor the situation. Government's most important tasks—national security, disaster relief, war—were systematically being handed off to others. The Oversight Committee issued a report in 2007 showing that spending on private contractors had more than doubled under President Bush, from $203.1 billion in 2000 to $412.1 billion in 2006, while no-bid contracts had tripled, from $67.5 billion to $206.9 billion. Government auditors had identified 187 contracts during those six years—valued at $1.1 trillion—as being plagued by overcharges, wasteful spending, or mismanagement.

*   *   *

ONE OF THE GREAT FRUSTRATIONS OF LIFE IN THE MINORITY IS that the rules don't offer many ways of blocking the kind of investigations that were Burton's specialty. Majority power, especially in the House, is near absolute. But that doesn't mean there aren't constructive ways for members in the other party to agitate on issues that really do deserve investigation. An important lesson from the early years of the Clean Air fight was that even if you lack the strength to pass a good law, great benefits can derive merely from getting important information before the public. The most we could manage in 1985 was the Toxic Release Inventory; but the data this later produced, documenting the enormous level of airborne pollution, shifted the legislative debate and became a big step toward a landmark law. Similarly, while we couldn't stop Burton, we could, even from the minority, compile a public record on neglected issues that needed congressional oversight.

We realized early in Burton's tenure that there was no point in spending all our time and staff resources responding to what he wanted to do. After the Hubbell affair, his investigations stopped gaining traction, so we devoted more and more time to addressing problems that urgently needed government attention. House precedent allots the minority one-third of the committee's substantial budget and staff. Although I didn't control the gavel, and therefore could not convene hearings, nothing was stopping us from conducting our own investigations of the issues we deemed important and making the findings public. While this method didn't carry the televisual oomph of a high-profile hearing, our reports did carry the imprimatur of the U.S. Congress, and that was a pretty big deal—often enough to make the kind of impact that brings meaningful change.

Our first report looked into the rising price of prescription drugs. Drawing on data from a number of federal agencies, the staff determined that uninsured seniors routinely had to pay more than twice as much for drugs as HMOs and other large purchasers. Tom Allen, a Maine Democrat, took a particular interest. High drug prices were a major issue for his constituents, given their proximity to Canada and its lower prices, and Allen asked if we could tailor a report to his district. We did, and it became the lead story on the local news. Democrats Jim Turner of Texas and Tom Udall of New Mexico requested reports for their districts, and got a similar reception. Word spread quickly, and soon dozens of members were asking for their own "Waxman Reports," as they became known. District-by-district comparisons of high drug prices began showing up in newspapers across the country. Turner convinced President Clinton to include the issue in his 1999 State of the Union address, which added to the momentum. The movement to create a Medicare prescription drug benefit originated not in Washington but at the grass roots. It was partly energized, I believe, by these reports.

The amount of attention frankly surprised us. Several members told me that nothing they had done in their career had generated as much interest as publicizing their local findings. So we decided to expand our product line.

We were soon pumping out reports comparing U.S. drug prices to those in England and Canada, and others comparing the cost of drugs used on humans with veterinary drugs (veterinarians often used the same drugs at a dramatically lower cost). Then we branched out into reports on classroom overcrowding and nursing home abuses. Many of these studies were produced at the request of Democratic members, but we also conducted investigations for Republicans who recognized their value. We joined with Republican senator Susan Collins of Maine to examine the involuntary incarceration of mentally ill youths. Our work for Representative Steven Largent, an Oklahoma Republican, made national headlines for revealing that online file-sharing programs bombarded kids with pornography. All told, the minority staff produced more than one thousand individual reports during my tenure as ranking member.

Through these creative and roundabout means, we managed to keep up some oversight during the twelve obstinate years that Republicans reigned over the House. But these were stopgap measures that couldn't possibly do the job of a fully engaged and active committee, and I often longed for the day when Democrats would regain power.

WHEN THAT DAY FINALLY ARRIVED IN JANUARY 2007, I TOOK OVER as chairman of the Oversight Committee. Having witnessed so much abuse of power and so much neglected responsibility from our days in the minority, my Democratic colleagues and I were determined to right the ship. We settled on a three-part approach. First, we would concentrate on pursuing fraud, waste, and abuse of resources. Second, we would ensure that government was working as it should be, taking particular care to examine the agencies that had declined most precipitously under President Bush, such as the Federal Emergency Management Agency—FEMA—which had performed so poorly during Hurricane Katrina. And lastly, we would once again hold the executive branch accountable for its performance, as the Constitution requires. The excesses of the Burton years and the neglect during Bush's presidency had done plenty to harm the country, but also furnished us with a powerful model of how not to behave.

To convey to a disillusioned country how much change we had in mind, my staff and I worked overtime as the new Congress approached so that we could get going quickly. We opened with four consecutive days of oversight hearings, each day designed to highlight one of the more egregious examples of fraud, waste, and abuse that successive Republican Congresses had ignored.

On Tuesday, February 6, we examined an audit report from the Special Inspector General for Iraq Reconstruction that revealed that $8.8 billion—literally 363 tons in shrink-wrapped packages of $100 bills—had been flown into Iraq on 230 military cargo planes, delivered to the Coalition Provisional Authority, and had gone missing. It had been handed out to Iraqi officials with no record of who got what or where it went. The man responsible, Bush's former CPA administrator, L. Paul Bremer, admitted that the money had simply vanished.

On Wednesday, February 7, we looked at Blackwater USA, the private military contractor accused of profiteering by the families of four Blackwater employees who had been lynched in Fallujah and their bodies burned and dragged through the streets, a horror videotaped and broadcast worldwide. The hearing revealed that Blackwater had failed to provide armored vehicles and skirted critical safety measures, at the cost of U.S. lives. This spurred the Army to withhold $19.6 million from Halliburton, which had subcontracted with Blackwater to provide armed security guards.

On Thursday, February 8, we held a hearing on the mismanagement of major Homeland Security Department projects outsourced to private contractors, including the Coast Guard's Deepwater program, which had produced ships that couldn't stay afloat. It turned out that managers of the Coast Guard's $24 billion fleet overhaul program had covered up a Navy engineering report that showed that design flaws in the flagship cutter slated to become the cornerstone of the Coast Guard's new fleet could cause the hull to buckle. Fixing each of the faulty vessels doubled the cost to taxpayers from $517 million to $1 billion. The report concluded that the problems had arisen from a fundamental lack of oversight.

On Friday, February 9, we turned to drug company profiteering through systematically overcharging government health programs like Medicare, Medicaid, and the Public Health Service, at a cost of billions of dollars. By law, drug companies must offer Medicaid their lowest prices, but they had repeatedly conspired to get around this requirement. Companies including Pfizer, Schering-Plough, GlaxoSmithKline, Astra Zeneca, and Bayer had to pay billions of dollars in civil damages and criminal penalties to federal and state governments.

Over the next two years, we returned again and again to the theme of wasteful spending, uncovering abuses that saved taxpayers billions of dollars. Having documented waste in the federal crop insurance program, we worked with the House Agriculture Committee to cut more than $3 billion in unnecessary subsidies. After we demonstrated that private insurers had overcharged the government by more than $600 million to provide workers' compensation coverage in Iraq, we joined with the House Armed Services Committee to close the loophole.

And this was only the beginning. Other hearings prompted further long-overdue reforms. We revealed that FEMA was housing families displaced by Hurricane Katrina in trailers with dangerous levels of formaldehyde—and that after field workers alerted the agency's leaders in Washington they were instructed to ignore the threat, since verifying the trailers' toxicity "would imply FEMA's ownership of this issue." The ensuing public outrage got the families into safer shelter. A hearing with the head of Blackwater highlighted the company's reckless, shoot-first practices, and brought new controls on private security contractors in Iraq.

At the same time, we were seeking to make top government officials accountable. Lurita Doan, head of the General Services Administration, had tried to divert agency resources to help elect Republicans in close races, and Howard Krongard, the State Department's inspector general, had stymied an investigation into Blackwater, on whose advisory board his own brother served (which he denied under oath). Both officials were forced from office. We also established, and let the country know, that dozens of top White House staffers were evading the requirements of the Presidential Records Act and shielding their e-mail from scrutiny by using outside accounts. And in two of the highest-profile hearings of the Bush presidency, we laid out how senior White House officials had revealed the identity of a covert CIA agent, Valerie Plame, and investigated why the Army sought to keep from the public and the family of Pat Tillman—the football hero turned Army Ranger after 9/11—that he had been killed by friendly fire while serving in Afghanistan.

THE OVERSIGHT COMMITTEE'S JURISDICTION IS NOT LIMITED TO government, extending to almost any area, including the private sector. Early in my chairmanship, we became deeply involved in investigating what would become the frightening collapse of the U.S. economy in the autumn of 2008.

What first caught our attention, well before the recession, was the issue of CEO pay. By the time I took over in 2007, the skyrocketing amounts being paid to executives of the nation's largest companies had begun to worry me, because it raised important questions about corporate governance: Not merely that the size of these payouts gave offense—some ranged higher than $100 million—but that they had become so enormous that they were skewing the way businesses operated.

In the 1980s, the CEOs of the nation's largest companies were paid forty times more than the average employee. By 2007 they were making about six hundred times more. At a typical company, a staggering 10 percent of corporate profits went to paying top executives. Many academic experts, financial analysts, and investors had come to regard this trend as the index of a fundamentally broken way of running a company. As Warren Buffett remarked, "In judging whether corporate America is serious about reforming itself, CEO pay remains the acid test." There seemed to be no serious signs of reform.

To get a better handle on what was happening, the committee staff conducted a broad survey of how the 250 largest companies established executive pay. They turned out to rely heavily on independent consultants specializing in executive compensation who routinely had a major conflict of interest— namely, that the bulk of their income derived from consulting for the very same executives whose salaries they set. Our report found that on average these supposedly disinterested consultants earned $200,000 to advise a company about executive pay and another $2 million to provide other services to the same company. So the bulk of the consultants' income depended upon the goodwill of the very CEOs they were being paid to overpay, an arrangement often hidden from shareholders. They were anything but "independent."

In December, we held a hearing to highlight the report's findings and examine this troubling practice. As a result of this, and of ensuing shareholder outcry, many companies announced that they would only hire consultants free of such conflicts.

But problems of corporate governance did not disappear. Early 2008 brought the subprime mortgage meltdown that eventually drove the American economy into collapse. To the disgust of people everywhere, the CEOs of some of the companies directly responsible for the mortgage mess received payouts of hundreds of millions of dollars, even as their firms lost billions. Here was a glaring example of lack of accountability, whose effects wound up touching nearly every American.

In March, we convened a hearing and invited three of them to testify: Charles O. Prince III, formerly chairman and CEO of Citigroup; Stanley O'Neal, formerly chairman and CEO of Merrill Lynch; and Angelo Mozilo, the founder and CEO of Countrywide Financial Corporation. Soon after the hearing was announced, I got a sense of just how influential these men were. Countrywide's headquarters is located in my district, and though I'd never met Angelo Mozilo, calls began to pour in from important people in California who tried to change my mind about having Mozilo testify or suggested that I postpone the hearing. Nancy Pelosi, the speaker of the house, was subjected to a similar barrage, but agreed that we should go forward.

The hearing sought to answer the question, How can a few executives do so well when their companies do so poorly? In 2007, the companies had lost a combined $20 billion, yet Mozilo collected $120 million; O'Neal $161 million; and Prince, who was actually fired, was still awarded $68 million and millions more in perquisites like a car and driver. Though each executive defended his pay, the hearing illustrated the massive lack of accountability on Wall Street and how its system of compensation contributed to the mortgage boom, while giving executives huge incentives to take the risks that eventually caused the mortgage market to implode.

By the time Congress returned from summer break, the economy was falling apart and Wall Street was being ravaged. By September, the Federal Reserve and the Treasury Department had narrowly averted a Bear Stearns bankruptcy, bailed out the insurance giant AIG for $85 billion, and let Lehman Brothers fail, freezing credit markets worldwide and necessitating the emergency $700 billion bailout known as the Troubled Asset Relief Program. Speaker Pelosi charged Barney Frank of Massachusetts, chairman of the House Financial

Services Committee, with putting together a bailout package, and asked me to conduct a series of hearings to find out how we had arrived at such a calamitous point. In October, as the global economy teetered on the verge of collapse, we held four high-profile hearings, each examining a different component of the disaster.

Our purpose was to find out why the financial system fell apart, where it broke down, and why regulators had been unable to warn us or stop it from happening. We began on October 6 and 7 with hearings that included Lehman Brothers CEO Richard Fuld, who had just presided over the largest bankruptcy in U.S. history, and Robert Willumstad and Martin Sullivan, the former CEOs of AIG, whose reckless trading in credit default swaps had put the entire U.S. economy at risk. Though Fuld refused to accept responsibility, blaming Lehman's failure on "a litany of destabilizing factors" beyond his control, the thousands of pages of internal documents that our investigators examined portrayed a culture where huge bonuses and the lack of any consequence for failure encouraged reckless, highly leveraged bets with billions of borrowed dollars that wiped the company out when housing prices started to drop. Even after destroying his firm, Fuld departed a rich man, having "earned" more than $500 million.

Like Lehman Brothers, AIG had grown mighty by taking excessive risks, in this case insuring other companies' investments by issuing "credit default swaps"—an unregulated $62 trillion market that AIG had pioneered—that it could not pay off when these investments went bad. And like Lehman Brothers, AIG's top executives earned hundreds of millions of dollars. In fact, the man most directly responsible for destroying the company, Joseph Cassano, head of its financial products division, received $280 million—and then, after being fired, was awarded $34 million in unvested bonuses and placed on a

$1 million-a-month retainer. Why would AIG keep him on the payroll? To subject him to a noncompete clause, the CEOs explained, so that he could not go to work for a competing firm.

This infuriating Wonderland logic was trumped only by the executives' arrogant refusal to change their ways. The week after the government had to give it $85 billion, AIG sponsored a lavish retreat at a San Diego spa. An alert constituent spotted an announcement in a local newspaper and called Karen Lightfoot, a committee staffer. Our investigators obtained billing invoices from the resort showing that AIG had spent $440,000 to house its executives in presidential suites at more than $1,000 per night, including $150,000 on food and $230,000 on spa treatments—all while being propped up on taxpayer dollars. News of the retreat dominated the next day's hearing and, for many Americans, crystallized the attitude of reckless entitlement that suffused Wall Street and led directly to the financial collapse.

Our hearings then broadened to the credit rating agencies that had vouched for the toxic mortgage bonds and to the government regulators who enabled the speculation. On October 22, the CEOs of Moody's, Fitch, and Standard & Poor's, the firms that acted as gatekeepers by assigning quality ratings to bonds, appeared before the committee. Like the finance executives before them, they pleaded their innocence, claiming that, as Moody's CEO Ray McDaniel put it, "virtually no one . . . anticipated what is occurring." That turned out to be false.

Witnesses unhappy about testifying pursue a number of tactics to thwart our investigators. The ratings agencies tried to bury us in paper. A request for internal documents brought hundreds of thousands of pages just before the hearing, apparently in the hope that damning evidence would be impossible to find amid all the detritus. To meet this challenge, staff from every part of the committee dropped what they were doing to embark on an emergency document-reviewing marathon—an exercise that paid off.

To Ray McDaniel at the witness table, we were able to show that someone had indeed anticipated exactly what was occurring as the subprime bubble inflated: McDaniel himself. In a confidential presentation in October 2007, he had warned his board of directors that in their unbridled pursuit of revenue, the ratings agencies were competing to give high ratings to risky bonds, sacrificing standards for money. This "dilemma," McDaniel had warned, posed a "very tough problem" for the company. "Unchecked, competition on this basis can place the entire financial system at risk." And indeed, it did. As another Moody's executive put it, "We sold our soul to the devil for revenue."

Here again was a blatant and deadly conflict of interest. The credit rating agencies were paid by the bond *issuers* rather than bond *buyers*—which gave them, like the executive compensation consultants, an overwhelming incentive to please the firms that supplied their handsome revenues, rather than to issue objective assessments of bond quality, as they were supposed to. Hundreds of billions of dollars of risky subprime mortgage bonds were thus passed off as AAA-rated safe investments. And when it turned out otherwise, the disparity brought on a global recession.

Our pivotal hearing came the next day, October 23, when Alan Greenspan, the legendary former head of the Federal Reserve, joined other regulators to explain how the government had failed to prevent the crisis. Since the Reagan years, the prevailing attitude in Washington had been that the market always knew best. The Federal Reserve had the authority to stop the irresponsible lending practices that fueled the subprime market, but Greenspan rejected pleas to intervene. The SEC could have demanded higher credit rating standards, but did not. The Treasury Department could have forced better over-sight of financial derivatives, but declined to. The deregulatory philosophy that marked the age became so powerful that it trumped governance. A point was reached when nothing kept the markets honest.

When my turn came to ask questions, I quoted some of Greenspan's views on regulation, such as the claim that "There's nothing involved in federal regulation which makes it superior to market regulation." My question for him was simply "Were you wrong?"

"Partially," he replied.

When I later pursued the point, I asked directly, "Well, where did you make a mistake, then?"

"I made a mistake in presuming that the self-interest of orga-nizations, specifically banks and others, were such as that they were best capable of protecting their own shareholders and their equity in the firms."

A moment later, he went further.

"What I am saying to you is, yes, I found a flaw, I don't know how significant or permanent it is, but I have been very dis-tressed by that fact."

"You found a flaw?"

"I found a flaw in the model that I perceived is the critical functioning structure that defines how the world works, so to speak."

"In other words, you found that your view of the world, your ideology, was not right, it was not working?"

"Precisely. That's precisely the reason I was shocked, be-cause I had been going for forty years or more with very con-siderable evidence that it was working exceptionally well."

Greenspan's testimony reverberated around the globe. The man regarded as the high priest of high finance—"The

Maestro"—had candidly admitted that unfettered markets and lax regulation had been principal causes of the collapse. It was something that no one had expected, a gravely fitting coda to our hearings, and a bookend of sorts to the Age of Reagan that had now drawn to its end.

THE RECKLESS GREED OF WALL STREET, THE REGULATORY FAIL-ures, and the extraordinary waste, fraud, and abuse uncovered in our hearings share a common origin. They all stem from an ideology that holds that government intervention is inherently harmful and private sector actions inherently good. Ultimately, Greenspan and Bush committed the same error of believing that the private sector, left unregulated, would act in the public interest. Halliburton, Blackwater, Lehman Brothers, AIG, the credit rating agencies, and even high government officials exploited this system to amass vast fortunes before the bottom fell out. The really monstrous injustice is that the CEOs keep their millions, while ordinary citizens bear the brunt of the economic collapse as workers, home owners, and savers foot the bill as taxpayers to clean it all up.

Along with its shocking waste and dangerous inefficiencies, this approach to governing is fundamentally out of step with the American people. Government has a basic obligation to safeguard the money it collects, and Congress plays a vital role in this process. But during the eight years of the Bush presidency and the twelve years that Republicans controlled the House of Representatives, the American public came to see a staggering disregard for government, and especially for government regulation.

But the tenet of Republican faith that insists government oversight and regulation is unwarranted and harmful was put to the ultimate test when the U.S. economy began to collapse in 2008. Suddenly, the drawbacks of allowing industry to regulate itself became apparent to all. The bankruptcy of this philosophy was ratified by the American people on Election Day 2008, when they sent Barack Obama, a Democrat, to the White House.

CHAPTER 9

The Tobacco Wars

PRACTICALLY FROM THE MOMENT I ARRIVED IN CONGRESS, the fight against tobacco has defined my career. For thirty-five years, I've used every lever of government at my disposal to wage this battle, and I've done so for one simple and compelling reason: Tobacco kills 440,000 people every year, which makes it the single greatest public health threat America has encountered over the last sixty years. And the fact that this deadly product is legal makes it harder to regulate, and all the more dangerous.

For decades, the tobacco industry managed to hide or downplay the devastating societal consequences wrought by the millions of people who smoke. Every day, tobacco kills as many people as would perish if two jumbo jets crashed—and it continues killing at this rate, day after day after day. By any rational standard the cost in lives, dollars, and lost productivity constitutes a national emergency. Yet when I came to Congress, the issue barely registered. I soon discovered why: The tobacco companies' amazing grip on Washington let them evade the scrutiny that every other industry had to endure. In 1979, as a reform-minded young chairman of the Health and Environment Subcommittee, I set out to stop this from being so. Some epidemics are beyond our control. But this one was entirely avoidable. The single most important step anyone could take to improve the nation's health would be to cut back tobacco use. But doing so entailed taking on the most powerful interest group in town.

The story of our decades-long effort to curb tobacco's deadly prevalence and its malign influence over Washington is a saga of struggle between public need and private interest. The particulars of this struggle illuminate the process whereby powerful private interests burrow deep into the heart of our system of government, not just entrenching themselves but acquiring the ability to manipulate that system from within. For years, the tobacco industry's adroit use of Washington power enabled it to flourish, all but impervious to regulation or oversight. Only the committed efforts of a handful of legislators, who pushed year after year, often grinding out only incremental gains, managed to change this. But the fact that we did so demonstrates that concerned politicians can, and often do, prevail against even the most daunting opposition. Above all, the tobacco fight shows how the government can better our national culture, in this case saving tens of thousands of lives and improving the lives of millions of others.

VIEWED FROM TODAY, TOBACCO'S STATUS IN THE 1970S SEEMS all but unimaginable. People smoked everywhere, and they smoked a lot—in meeting rooms, elevators, restaurants, theaters, and on trains, buses, and airplanes. Few protested this state of affairs, because we were all conditioned to think of smoking as utterly ordinary and acceptable behavior. Those who did protest quickly encountered the industry's might. No interest group in Washington loomed larger than Big Tobacco, which possessed a sophisticated understanding of the congressional process, as well as the means and ability to influence it.

The tobacco industry has historically been powerful in Congress because its regional representatives zealously protect its interests, and do so with great skill. This is no accident. Since the Energy and Commerce Committee has jurisdiction over tobacco, the industry has long encouraged newly elected members from tobacco-producing states (most of whom it helped to win office) to seek membership. Steering committees for both parties determine where members are assigned, so, mindful of the importance of seniority in Congress, the industry goes to work there, too, carefully tracking the steering committee's roster in order to pressure and influence those who actually place the new members. This strategy ensures that a steady stream of allies is always moving up the ladder of the most important committees and subcommittees. For many years, when sympathetic chairmen retired, they were often succeeded by people with identical views on tobacco. It was a measure of the industry's success on this front that the man I defeated in 1979 to become chairman of the Health and Environment Subcommittee—Richardson Preyer, a North Carolina Democrat—did not believe that tobacco was harmful.

When I got to Congress, the industry made little distinction between the parties. Most of the powerful chairmen in those days were Southern Democrats. But the industry spread money around to both leaderships, and curried additional favor—and gained unparalleled access—by shrewdly alleviating one of the most tedious aspects of a congressman's life: the constant travel on commercial airliners. The tobacco companies routinely shuttled congressmen around the country in corporate jets. (When I later challenged this practice, my own party's leadership was as cool to the idea as the Republicans'.) Tobacco companies always ranked among the largest contributors of "soft money" to the party committees, funded lavish inaugural balls, and happily underwrote the annual galas for more charity foundations than you could imagine—all of which bought them unexpected allies, and silenced some who might otherwise have spoken up.

The industry understood its vulnerabilities and carefully purchased protection. Smoking kills minorities at a disproportionate rate. So tobacco companies funneled disproportionately large sums to minority-heavy districts through grants to local schools, charities, arts foundations, and other community projects. These districts were often among the poorest in the country, and desperately needed the money. Consequently, their benefactors enjoyed outsized influence in the very communities that suffered the most harm from their products.

This is how tobacco came to wield such enormous clout, not just in Congress but throughout Washington. The industry effectively stood beyond the reach of the federal government. The Food and Drug Administration lacked the authority to regulate tobacco. The Consumer Product Safety Commission was explicitly forbidden to oversee tobacco and guns. And the Federal Trade Commission's authority only extended as far as misleading advertising claims, which wasn't far at all. Needless to say, neither party particularly wanted to change this sorry state of affairs. The tobacco industry was close to impregnable.

But even this protection and influence could not eliminate the mounting evidence of what tobacco was doing to millions of Americans. So the industry devised two very successful methods of staving off attempts at reform. The first was to encourage the idea that it was natural and acceptable to smoke. Cigarette companies hired the best minds on Madison Avenue to portray smokers as attractive, athletic, successful types engaged in a "lifestyle" that others would want to emulate, a notion that they reinforced by sponsoring athletic events (the Virginia Slims women's tennis tour, the NASCAR Winston Cup) and creating iconic corporate mascots like Joe Camel and the Marlboro Man that were designed to be cultural signifiers of cool. The campaign to transform a destructive habit into seemingly wholesome behavior went beyond advertising. Underwriting philanthropic and charitable activities lent tobacco companies a sheen of civic-mindedness, allowing them to masquerade as stewards of the culture and pillars of the community, rather than merchants whose products caused death and disease. In Washington, their efforts to pass themselves off as a respected part of the establishment were pervasive—and even I was not immune.

Like many politicians, I have a dirty secret: I used to smoke. In high school, I would tool around West Los Angeles in my green-and-white Buick, dragging on a cigarette and imagining myself the epitome of cool. With considerable effort, I quit smoking after college, prompted by the emerging medical consensus that tar and nicotine were dangerous carcinogens. But early in my congressional tenure, I relapsed. It happened on a CODEL, the Washington acronym for "congressional delegation," or one of the formal trips that congressmen take together on business. Everywhere I turned, cigarettes were being provided gratis to the members of our party—on the plane, in the hotel. It was all part of the industry effort to gull official Washington into feeling comfortable about smoking. To be sociable, I decided to light up, and because I hadn't smoked in a long time, it packed a punch. Somehow, I convinced myself that I could smoke now and then without falling back into the habit. Before long, I was hooked again—and mortified to be so, since I was already becoming known as a crusader against tobacco.

Driven by a deep sense of embarrassment, I managed to quit for good. I rejoined the ranks of ex-smokers, chastened and with a profound appreciation for the tobacco industry's wily influence.

The second way the industry staved off reform was by going to any length to create uncertainty about whether smoking was truly harmful. Though respectable doctors and scientists were nearly unanimous in agreeing that it was, the tobacco companies hired their own doctors and scientists to churn out study after study suggesting otherwise. The industry erected pseudo-scientific front groups like the Council for Tobacco Research to cast doubts on any connection between smoking and disease, while its armies of lawyers labored to ensure that no court of law would find a tobacco company liable for dying smokers' health claims. Flimsy though it was, this "scientific evidence" armed tobacco's allies with sufficient deniability to maintain tobacco's socially acceptable status. This helped discourage the idea that a culture of pervasive smoking was anything other than ordinary, which in turn made any efforts to curb smoking seem like a faddish cause for slightly nutty do-gooders.

All this elaborate effort was necessary for the companies to escape government oversight. Smoking was framed as a personal choice, a private matter in which the government had no place interfering. For years, the industry pushed the line that if people chose to smoke, well, that was their business. No one had the right to tell them otherwise. This argument long proved effective. But it rested on an assurance that tobacco did no harm to anyone who had not themselves chosen to smoke. The industry insistently raised doubts about every new scientific study linking tobacco to cancer, partly to keep its own customers from quitting, but also because its laissez-faire argument would break down overnight if the public came to realize the dangers of secondhand smoke.

*   *   *

MAJOR ACHIEVEMENTS IN CONGRESS ARE RARELY REACHED OVER A single session. Tobacco's clout and benign public image meant that significant reform would be especially difficult to bring about. Realistically, we had no hope of persuading Congress to regulate tobacco in the near term. So instead we turned to the oversight process as a way to begin pushing back against tobacco's carefully constructed edifice and dramatize the alarming health effects that the industry worked so hard to obscure.

We certainly did not lack for evidence. Scientists had established as long ago as 1953 that tobacco caused cancer in rats. A year later, researchers linked smoking to lung cancer, heart disease, and a general increase in the death rate. In 1964, a landmark surgeon general's report concluded that cigarette smoking caused cancer, and soon afterward Congress had required that cigarette packages carry warning labels. But little headway had been made against smoking since then, even as the staggering toll on public health continued to mount. In 1979, smoking was killing 400,000 people a year, and yet the industry could still deny that its product killed anyone.

Beginning in the early 1980s, I chaired a series of subcommittee hearings designed to bring these facts to light. Over several years, we brought in celebrities from Miss America to Captain Kangaroo to talk about the dangers of smoking, and to emphasize the rate of death and disease, the loss of productivity, and the family tragedies that invariably befall heavy smokers. While the celebrities did draw media attention, the coverage of the issues they testified about tended to dissipate quickly, making it difficult to sustain our campaign.

One area where we found some traction was in arguing for stronger cigarette warning labels. The label Congress had settled on in 1965 asserted vaguely that smoking was "harmful" to one's health, which rather understated the case. Almost twenty years later, the message had become timeworn and long since lost whatever effectiveness it might have possessed. By hammering away at the dangers of tobacco in our hearings, we persuaded Congress to pass a law in 1984 that mandated new, more sharply worded, and much larger warning labels that rotated over time and linked cigarette smoking to specific ailments like lung cancer, heart disease, and emphysema. The law also extended the labeling requirement to billboards, newspapers, and other modes of advertising. Even so, the industry extracted a concession on what it considered a crucial issue of terminology: The link between smoking and disease could not be presented on the warning labels as an empirical fact, but instead was attributed to the surgeon general—thereby preserving the sliver of deniability the industry relied on.

Smokeless tobacco was another area that had escaped regulation, to tragic effect among the young men who were its core users. Snuff and chewing tobacco were exempt from labeling requirements, leading many kids to conclude erroneously that these products did not cause cancer. Sean Marsee, a high school track and field star from Oklahoma, was one such user who became the focus of a hearing on smokeless tobacco's deadly effects. Marsee had started dipping Copenhagen snuff as a twelve-year-old. One day he discovered what turned out to be a cancerous red sore on his tongue, the size of a half dollar. His tongue was cut out, but the cancer still spread to his lymph nodes, necessitating several more disfiguring surgeries that could not, in the end, save his life. Soon after he died in 1984, at the age of nineteen, we introduced legislation extending the warning label requirement to smokeless tobacco. Surgeon General C. Everett Koop became an important ally, testifying that tobacco use among children was increasing, evidently in response to the industry's multimillion-dollar advertising blitz featuring popular athletes and entertainers. In 1986, we succeeded in getting warning labels on smokeless tobacco products and prohibiting broadcast advertising for them.

Progress came slowly. But as scientific studies kept widening the range of health problems caused by tobacco, we continued to highlight the findings in oversight hearings. The purpose, as always, was to raise awareness that might lead to better laws and stronger regulation. One particular focus was the effect of secondhand smoke. During the 1980s, a number of studies began to amplify its dangers—demonstrating, for instance, that nonsmoking spouses of heavy smokers develop lung cancer at far higher rates that other nonsmokers, and that babies whose mothers smoke developed infections and diseases far more readily than those whose mothers didn't. In 1986, Koop authored the first surgeon general's report devoted to examining the effects of secondhand smoke. He concluded that "it is now clear that disease risk due to inhalation of tobacco smoke is not solely limited to the individual who is smoking, but can also extend to those individuals who inhale tobacco smoke in room air." This was the news the tobacco industry feared. But while our hearings called attention to these findings, the initial results did not materialize in Washington, where the industry maintained a hammerlock, but at the state and local levels, prompting hundreds of anti-smoking ordinances in municipalities across the country.

In 1987, Representative Richard Durbin, an Illinois Democrat, finally forced the issue in Congress by introducing an amendment to the Federal Aviation Act banning smoking on airplane flights shorter than two hours. Durbin, the son of a two-pack-a-day smoker who died of lung cancer when he was fourteen, knew he faced an uphill battle. His proposal was opposed by the Transportation Department, then twice defeated in the House, first in an Appropriations subcommittee and again in the full committee. Only deft maneuvering and an assist from Claude Pepper of Florida, the chairman of the Rules Committee (who had helped create the National Cancer Institute as a senator in the 1930s), brought the Durbin amendment to the House floor and presented the first direct challenge to tobacco's dominion.

The floor debate was a microcosm of the larger fight over tobacco. Supporters of the amendment, including me, emphasized the overwhelming scientific consensus about the dangers of secondhand smoke: the National Academy of Sciences, the American Cancer Society, and the surgeon general all agreed. Furthermore, polls showed that two-thirds of Americans supported a smoking ban on airplanes. The industry's allies threw up every obstacle they could, arguing against the amendment on grounds of procedure (it had been defeated in subcommittee), cost of compliance (an industry group ginned up the figure of $613 million), safety (desperate addicts would surreptitiously smoke in airplane lavatories, creating "an onboard fire hazard"), complacency ("If it ain't broke, don't fix it"), and even, oddly enough, constitutionality ("It seems to me that under our Constitution," Representative Dan Daniel of Virginia argued, "under our form of government, our philosophy, that if a person wants to smoke, they have the right to do that"). Others resorted to ridicule and scare tactics. Tom DeLay of Texas warned that "a smoking patrol" would "interrogate passengers" as they disembarked. Jim Bunning of Kentucky conjured up Orwellian squads of "smoke sniffers" crawling through airplanes to hunt for rogue puffers.

It was a reflection of tobacco's power, of how thoroughly the industry had conditioned Americans to accept the ubiquity of cigarette smoking, that being forced to sit for hours in a big metal tube and breathe other people's tobacco smoke needed to be debated at length on the floor of Congress. But as voting began, the outcome was very much in doubt. In the end, the Durbin amendment squeezed through by a single vote (the final tally being 198-193 after several members switched sides to keep up appearances once the outcome became clear) to everyone's surprise, including Durbin's.

NOT UNTIL 1993 DID WE ACHIEVE A BREAKTHROUGH THAT TRULY began to shift the balance of power. Our greatest difficulty in battling the tobacco industry had been our frustrating inability to find out what was happening on the inside. A veil of silence shrouded and protected the industry, which forced its employees, including scientists and researchers, to sign nondisclosure agreements that forbade them from revealing any internal information. But a handful had quietly begun to talk.

A convergence of several factors that year convinced our team that the time had come to intensify our campaign. The EPA had just released a comprehensive risk assessment of secondhand smoke certifying its carcinogenic qualities and revealing that children were at especially high risk. The report concluded that secondhand smoke was a "Class A" carcinogen like asbestos, arsenic, and benzene that caused three thousand lung cancer deaths each year. In response, we introduced legislation banning smoking in restaurants and federal buildings. Around the same time, David Kessler, the FDA commissioner so outspoken about the dangers of dietary supplements, announced plans to consider regulating cigarettes as a drug, after learning that the tobacco companies were manipulating nicotine levels to addict more smokers. Along with Congress and the federal agencies, the news media, too, had renewed their interest in Big Tobacco, delivering several penetrating investigations, none more illuminating than a *Wall Street Journal* series entitled "Smoke and Mirrors" that documented the industry's "massive effort to cast doubt on the links between smoking and disease" by creating and funding entire organizations devoted to manufacturing bogus scientific research. The Health and Environment Subcommittee became a kind of clearinghouse for emerging information, as we held hearing after hearing and issued reports that drove the issue ever closer to the center of public attention.

Visibility brings sources. As stories about our oversight hearings appeared more and more frequently in newspapers and on television, a handful of researchers and scientists who had done work for tobacco companies got in touch with the committee and provided the first glimpse behind tobacco's iron wall. What they described was often astonishing: tests on children to see how they reacted to tobacco smoke; cigarette advertising designed to hook children in order to capture their "brand loyalty" early in life; a South American laboratory where company scientists experimented with gene manipulation to produce a tobacco plant with a higher level of nicotine. One particularly helpful informant, a former research scientist at Philip Morris named Victor DeNoble, described to us how he had conducted comprehensive studies in the 1980s that demonstrated nicotine addiction and tolerance in rats—studies that Philip Morris had, in fact, twice forbidden him to publish. The company continued to insist publicly that its products were not addictive. This knowledge strengthened our resolve and helped guide our investigations and hearings. But the nondisclosure agreements prevented our sources from testifying or supplying the government with documentary evidence. We needed to find a way to share what they were telling us with the American public.

OVER AND ABOVE OUR INABILITY TO CALL THESE SCIENTISTS AND researchers as witnesses, an abiding frustration of the oversight hearings was the witnesses the industry did put forward. These were the highly compensated "experts" stationed at industry front groups like the Tobacco Institute and the Council for Tobacco Research whose work was bought and paid for precisely so that when Congress took up the issue of smoking it could be claimed that scientists remained uncertain as to whether tobacco had deadly effects. Although these fraudulent experts were always offset by our own legitimate ones, the very nature of a congressional hearing and its coverage in the news media creates a false equivalency that muddies the question of truth. Both sides tend to be treated equally, regardless of merit—which is, of course, precisely what the industry always counted on.

It was always clear to us that a major reason why the tobacco industry got away with such patent deception was because it operated through just these sorts of carefully chosen prox- ies. Tobacco had the best spokespeople, lawyers, lobbyists, ad men, and corporate icons that money could buy. This allowed the industry to hide the truth: that the very wealthy and pow- erful CEOs who controlled the seven major tobacco companies preyed on millions of people, including children, to generate ever larger profits at an enormous cost to society. The vast gulf between tobacco's myth and its reality was maintainable only because the American public had never been made to confront this disparity. We became convinced that the key to shattering tobacco's public image and exposing the industry for what it really was (a necessary precursor to any serious reform) lay in setting up just such a confrontation.

By the spring of 1994, the collective weight of congressio- nal investigations, oversight hearings, and pending legislation, along with Kessler's efforts at the FDA, had thrust the tobacco industry into the unaccustomed position of being on the de- fensive. Getting a significant bill through Congress remained an unlikely proposition. But the weight of public opinion was beginning to swing against the industry. Americans were particularly repelled by the charge that tobacco companies were spiking the nicotine level in cigarettes to induce addiction—a turn of affairs that frightened the industry sufficiently that it filed a $10 billion libel suit against ABC News for its reports on the subject.

To force the issue, we invited Kessler to testify before the subcommittee about nicotine spiking. He appeared on March 25, 1994, to state that he considered cigarettes to be "high-technology nicotine delivery systems"—drugs, in other words—that warranted FDA regulation. In riveting testimony, he described the intricate methods by which tobacco companies controlled nicotine delivery, punching tiny holes in cigarette filters, for instance, to make "inhalation" more difficult for the smoking machines that government scientists use to measure tar—holes that an actual smoker would cover with his lips or fingers, thereby increasing the potency of the smoke and the amount of tar inhaled. Having put these public charges into play, I thanked him for his testimony, and, noting that the industry denied these claims, I issued a very public invitation to the seven tobacco company CEOs to appear before the subcommittee and offer a rebuttal. To raise the stakes even further, we announced that they would be the only witnesses invited to testify—and made clear that the hearing would be held whether or not they agreed to appear. If they chose not to avail themselves of the opportunity, the television cameras would capture seven empty chairs, leaving the public to draw its own conclusions about whether the tobacco industry had something to hide.

THERE WAS NO REASON, NO VALID ARGUMENT TO MAKE, FOR WHY they could not present themselves. The *New York Times* editorialized in favor of the idea, adding to the steadily growing pressure. Ultimately, they agreed to testify before the subcommittee on April 14.

For all the clamor, they probably did not regard the hearing as a serious threat, and certainly not as the pivotal moment that it wound up becoming. To all outward appearances, in fact, it hardly seemed a fair fight: a subcommittee chairman and his handful of allies against the most formidable industry Washington had known in forty years, its legions of high-priced lawyers and fixers filling up the gallery behind the seven powerful men at the witness table.

My own belief is that the CEOs viewed the hearing not as a threat but as an opportunity. The proceedings were taking place against a backdrop of growing populist anger at Washington and the Democratic Party that controlled it. Driven by aggressive Republican leaders like Newt Gingrich and Tom DeLay, momentum was already building toward what would become a historic rout in the midterm elections seven months hence that would deliver Congress to the Republicans. The popular Republican charge that Democrats favored intrusive big government was one the tobacco companies eagerly adopted, portraying their executives as victims of a power-addled chairman bent upon taking away everybody's cigarettes. But as the CEOs stood in a row to be sworn in, they were unprepared to be confronted by facts rather than partisan ideology.

My staff and many of the members most closely aligned with us had spent weeks preparing for the showdown. We had organized the hearing around four issues that would be the focus of relentless questioning: What were the health effects of smoking cigarettes? Did the tobacco companies believe nicotine was addictive? Did they market cigarettes to children? Did they manipulate the nicotine level in their products?

Over the next seven hours, under the full glare of the spot-light, the CEOs testified together for the first time. Their strug-gle to provide compelling answers to these questions and the self-evidently false nature of so much of their testimony forever changed the way that Americans view the tobacco companies. At every turn, they denied that cigarettes were addictive, and yet readily admitted that they would prefer their own children not to smoke. The inconsistencies were plain for all to see.

One of the day's most starkly memorable exchanges oc-curred between me and Andrew H. Tisch, chairman and chief executive of the Lorillard Tobacco Company, who had stated in an earlier sworn deposition that he did not believe cigarettes caused cancer. I asked him again whether he knew that ciga-rettes caused cancer.

"I do not believe that," he replied.

"Do you understand how isolated you are from the scientific community in your belief?"

"I do, sir."

The tobacco executives also denied marketing to children. Hearing this, Mike Synar of Oklahoma displayed an advertis-ing poster that showed Joe Camel in a nightclub surrounded by young people who were hanging out and smoking. Synar pressed the executives repeatedly to explain who the ad was intended to reach, if not kids. As the back-and-forth proceeded, people could see the facts for themselves simply by looking at the poster. The CEOs' positions became harder and harder to defend.

Our plan for the day was to extract more than just testi-mony. A high-profile hearing temporarily shifts the balance of power, presenting opportunities to those with the presence of mind to exploit them. Drawing out the CEOs gave us a brief tactical advantage by eliminating the lawyers and public rela-tions types ordinarily in a position to run interference. It exposed the decision makers themselves, and did so on a public stage that limited their ability to dissemble. Synar used this advantage to spring a trap. Drawing on what we knew from Victor DeNoble, he asked William Campbell, the president and chief operating officer of Philip Morris, whether the company, despite its earlier denials, had indeed suppressed DeNoble's study showing that laboratory animals could become addicted to nicotine. Campbell admitted that it had. Synar pressed further. In light of this news, would the company agree to waive DeNoble's secrecy agreement and allow him to testify about his work? Campbell at first tried to hedge, replying that he'd have to check with the company's lawyers to see if that would be possible. Synar wouldn't relent, pointing out that Campbell, as the head of the company, had the final say. With the cameras rolling, it became impossible to hold out. Campbell was trapped. He reluctantly agreed to let DeNoble testify, setting the stage for the next act of the drama.

By day's end, each of the tobacco chiefs had agreed, however grudgingly, to provide Congress with extensive, previously secret research that their companies had performed on nicotine addiction in humans and animals.

THE CEOS DID NOT SUBMIT MEEKLY TO OUR CHARGES. WHAT THE "anti-tobacco industry wants is prohibition," James W. Johnston, chairman and chief executive of R. J. Reynolds Tobacco Company, declared in his testimony. Accusations of prohibitionist fanaticism filled the air, even though tobacco's opponents, myself included, had repeatedly stated that, while we did support regulating cigarettes and wanted to find ways to lessen the health and safety dangers they posed, we had no intention of seeking to ban them outright.

In the days that followed the hearing, the industry went back on the offensive, marshaling the full strength of its forces to push back against the congressional "witch hunt." But the charge never really gained traction. Big Tobacco seemed to have lost its grip on its own public image. The iconic picture of the seven CEOs being sworn in supplanted, in most people's minds, the ad-generated myth that the industry had so brilliantly carried off for so long. And the impoverished arguments the executives had put forth at the hearing—Reynolds claimed that cigarettes were no more addictive than Twinkies—collapsed of their own weight. We had accomplished our primary purpose: The industry's image was indelibly stained.

The new face of the industry—its *real* face—was that of executives in suits denying that cigarettes caused disease, denying that nicotine was addictive, denying having manipulated nicotine levels in cigarettes, and denying that they targeted kids—each of which turned out to be untrue. The hearing was a frontal assault on all that the industry had built up, and afterward it could no longer sustain the ruse. The very concessions that the CEOs granted us, waiving DeNoble's secrecy pact and agreeing to turn over internal documents, became the seeds of the industry's undoing, getting into the public record a massive chronicle of decades of harm and deception.

Even as the CEOs were testifying, the calls started pouring into our office from industry insiders outraged that their executives would so blatantly lie. Some of the most important witnesses against the industry, including Jeffrey Wigand, the vice president of research and development for the Brown & Williamson Tobacco Company, whose story was the basis for the hit movie *The Insider*, came forward after watching the hearing.

Two weeks after the CEOs testified, Victor DeNoble and his research partner, Paul Mele, appeared before the subcommittee to discuss their work for Philip Morris on the pharmacology of nicotine and its addictiveness in animals. Armed with graphic pictures, they described experiments in which rats were taught to depress levers that administered an intravenous injection of nicotine, how they gradually developed a tolerance that demanded ever greater amounts to achieve the same effect, and how they finally chose their nicotine fix over water. DeNoble testified that this research suggested that nicotine was addictive "on a level comparable to cocaine," a conclusion that completely contradicted the testimony given by his own company's CEO just days earlier.

Soon after that, we received secret documents from inside Hill & Knowlton, the formidable public relations firm retained by the tobacco industry's trade association, showing how the industry had known for decades that tobacco caused cancer and had embarked on an elaborate disinformation campaign rather than come forward with the truth. The committee released this information to the public.

A week after that, Mississippi's attorney general, Mike Moore, turned over internal documents from Brown & Williamson provided by an informant in the state's class action suit against the tobacco companies. The documents revealed that the company had known about tobacco's harmful effects and addictive nature for decades. They included a 1963 memo by Brown & Williamson's general counsel that stated: "We are, then, in the process of selling nicotine, an addictive drug." This blatantly contradicted the testimony given by Brown & Williamson's CEO, Thomas Sandefur, at the April 14 hearing, prompting us to schedule another hearing to determine whether Sandefur had knowingly lied to Congress. Brown & Williamson had other ideas. The company sued me and Representative Wyden in a Kentucky circuit court to reclaim their leaked documents and shut down the investigation. A federal district court judge quashed the subpoenas, accusing Brown & Williamson of trying to "intimidate" Congress, and noting that the Constitution's speech and debate clause protects members from legal actions stemming from their official duties. Sandefur reappeared before the subcommittee on June 24, claiming not to have read the incriminating documents, and reiterated his belief that nicotine was not addictive. "I am entitled to express that view, even though it may differ from the opinions of others," he said.

With every new revelation, the industry's standing eroded a little further.

THEN, IN NOVEMBER, WE WERE DEALT A TREMENDOUS SETBACK. It came not from the tobacco industry but from the American voters, who swept the Republican Party into power, forcing me out of the subcommittee chairmanship and bringing the tobacco hearings to a sudden, grinding halt. The new Republican chairman of the House Energy and Commerce Committee was Tom Bliley of Virginia, sometimes referred to as "the congressman from Philip Morris" because the company's main manufacturing facility was located in his Richmond district. Bliley did not, needless to say, have a great deal of interest in carrying on our investigation.

But the momentum against tobacco had gathered enough strength that even this substantial shift of power could not stop it. Dozens of state lawsuits against the industry were moving forward. And although we were now operating from the minority, we continued to benefit from all that we had set in motion, receiving a series of internal tobacco company documents that we in turn released to the public. These included new examples of the companies' spiking the nicotine level in cigarettes and evidence of how they misled the Federal Trade Commission about tar levels.

In 1995, we obtained internal documents revealing that Philip Morris had conducted studies on children and tobacco smoke, going so far as to examine hyperactive third-graders to see if they were a potential market. We had found that children were a very effective way to dramatize the overall dangers of tobacco and shame its supporters into relenting, so this was a particularly important leak. But one problem with being in the minority was that we could no longer convene a hearing to publicize this dramatic news. Simply disclosing the documents at a press conference might have put us in legal jeopardy. The Constitution's speech and debate clause guaranteed protection for members only during sessions of Congress. It wasn't clear that a court would agree that press conferences constituted official House business, and the proven litigiousness of the tobacco industry suggested a high likelihood that it would test the proposition. So in order to make the documents public, I went to the House floor and read their entire contents into the Congressional Record. Afterward, with the media clamoring to discuss this important new information, I had to decline all press requests since nothing I said to reporters was assured of being protected speech.

In late 1997, we got hold of something even more explosive: internal reports and memoranda from the boardroom of R. J. Reynolds revealing that the company had for decades targeted children as young as thirteen years old to reverse its flagging sales. The documents laid out, from conception to fruition, the Joe Camel marketing campaign and the rationale behind it. In the 1970s, RJR's board of directors was concerned that its Camel brand was paling in popularity to Marlboro among the youngest smokers. Reports stamped "RJR SECRET" described how the company set out to win the kind of fierce brand loyalty that is usually established among lifetime smokers before age eighteen. "To ensure increased and longer-term growth for Camel Filter," warned a memo, "the brand must increase its share penetration among the 14-24 age group." The Joe Camel campaign aimed to "youthen" the brand's appeal—which the company's advertising agency described as "about as young as you can get"—debuted in France before moving to the United States in 1987. That same year R. J. Reynolds also created a specialty brand for the youth market, describing "Camel Wides" in a memo as a "wider-circumference nonmenthol cigarette targeted at the young adult male smoker (primarily 13-24-year-old male Marlboro smokers)."

At the April 1994 hearing, R. J. Reynolds's chairman and CEO, James Johnston had attacked members of the subcommittee for questioning him about whether his company marketed to children. "The charge that's always buried at the industry is you have to go out and recruit these new smokers, you just have to," Johnston had thundered. "And the answer is that would be the stupidest thing we can do. . . . *We do not market to children and will not!*"

From the very beginning, the purpose of the oversight hearings had been to build a public record and eventually create enough momentum in Congress and among the American public for legislation to mitigate the terrible health effects of tobacco. In 1979, when I became chairman of the subcommittee, the industry's power was such that this goal was widely regarded as a bit eccentric and certainly hopeless, a view that more or less prevailed for the next fifteen years.

But by 1996, the actions of Congress had dramatically changed public perception of the industry and made real the possibility that comprehensive tobacco legislation could soon be forthcoming. Meanwhile, the multitude of state lawsuits posed a serious financial threat. Tobacco still held enormous power in Washington. But the landscape had changed.

At the time, Tom Bliley and I had forged a successful legislative partnership, having just negotiated major bipartisan agreements on regulating pesticides and drinking water. It was an interesting coincidence that this fruitful collaboration had arisen between two men widely regarded as being, respectively, the most pro- and anti-tobacco members of Congress. But having found common purpose on other seemingly intractable problems, we decided to give tobacco a try, too.

Our negotiations for a comprehensive tobacco bill followed the same model as they had for the pesticide measure, utter secrecy of the proceedings guaranteeing both sides the political cover necessary to explore compromises. Only Newt Gingrich, the Republican speaker of the house, and Richard Gephardt, the Democratic minority leader, were kept apprised. Unlike pesticides, which we had resolved in a marathon three-day meeting, regulating tobacco was a subject so knotty and complex that our negotiations carried on for two years. Throughout it all, both Gingrich and Gephardt steadily encouraged us to continue.

Negotiations were complicated by the fact that, publicly, Bliley and I represented opposite sides of a contentious issue. Anyone who watched us square off at a tobacco hearing could have been forgiven for assuming that we were mortal enemies. We were not. Bliley believed deeply in his ideological positions, as I did, and defended them vehemently. But by sitting next to each other for so long, we had developed trust and respect for each other. Once, during my chairmanship, I expressed sympathy for the toll that I imagined the hearings must be taking on him. "You do what you have to do, Henry," he replied. Bliley didn't wink; he wasn't happy about the hearings. But he was a thorough professional who understood that you argue positions on the merits and don't make it personal, he knew exactly why the hearings were happening, and he was a true public servant, whatever the difference in opinions.

In 1998, we finally reached an agreement that would resolve all the major tobacco issues, including broad federal regulation, strict curbs on youth smoking, and much stronger limits on smoking in public places. The centerpiece was not some heavy-handed government mandate but a market-based enforcement mechanism designed to reduce teen smoking. Our idea was to conduct a broad survey to establish a baseline of which brands of cigarettes kids smoked and at what volume. The tobacco companies would then be required to reduce sales to kids, penalizing any brand that failed to do so with a higher tax. This would give the companies themselves the incentive to reduce sales rather than putting all their effort into finding a way around some new law. Democrats could support the idea because it would reduce smoking, especially among the most vulnerable population, along with the attendant costs to government. Republicans could support it because it was a market-based, rather than a regulatory, approach that didn't include the $2-a-pack tax then at issue in the Senate.

When Bliley told Gingrich, "I've got something with Henry," he was invited to make a presentation to the Republican leadership a few days later. But Gingrich and I were heavily embroiled on opposite sides of Dan Burton's ongoing crusade against President Clinton in the Government Reform Committee, and Gingrich had recently taken to the House floor to attack me for refusing to grant immunity to several witnesses Burton was eager to have testify. (I had responded with what I considered the obvious charge that Gingrich and Burton were engaged in a witch hunt.) The timing couldn't have been worse. At the meeting, Gingrich, who always nursed grudges, led the charge against the compromise, forbidding Bliley, a major committee chairman, even to call up the bill for consideration. Our hopes for a compromise ended right there.

WHILE THE FAILURE TO PUSH THROUGH A STRONG LAW WAS FRUS-trating, the risk that Congress might settle for a weak one became a real concern. In the summer of 1997, much to my surprise, a group of anti-tobacco activists led by Mississippi attorney general Mike Moore announced that they had reached a broad settlement with the tobacco companies resolving forty state lawsuits and eighteen class actions filed on behalf of individual smokers. The industry had agreed to pay $368 billion over twenty-five years to help offset the cost of treating smoking-related illnesses and fund anti-smoking programs, and also accepted bans on advertising figures like Joe Camel and the Marlboro Man. In exchange, the deal effectively barred the FDA from regulating nicotine and gave the industry what it wanted most: immunity from further legal liability. All that was left was for Congress to ratify the deal in the form of a new law.

The problem, as so many of us saw it, was that the agreement demanded far too little of the tobacco companies. The industry's payout amounted to about $15 billion a year, much of which would go toward paying attorneys' fees. Meanwhile, smoking imposed $100 billion a year in health care costs and, the National Center on Addiction and Substance Abuse at Columbia University estimated, would cost Medicare alone $800 billion over the next twenty years. By shielding the tobacco companies from liability, the agreement foreclosed the possibility of recouping these costs. The desire among plaintiffs' lawyers for a quick and lucrative settlement had produced something that struck me as thoroughly indefensible. As former Surgeon General Koop put it, "I think we've been snookered."

This was a worrisome prospect because outside advocacy groups like the American Cancer Society and the American Heart Association can powerfully affect the legislative process when they decide to push hard for something. Were they to join forces with the tobacco industry, the resulting bill would be difficult or impossible to stop.

Without the chairman's gavel, it was impossible to hold

a hearing that would call attention to the weakness of the agreement. Or, at least, doing so in Congress was impossible. As we debated how to proceed, some colleagues and I had an idea: Why not hold a hearing outside Congress and draw on the same prominent experts whose testimony we would have solicited had we been in the majority? Thus was established the Advisory Committee on Tobacco Policy and Public Health, an independent panel co-chaired by former FDA commissioner David Kessler and former Surgeon General Koop. A bipartisan group of legislators, myself included, asked this new panel to study the agreement and recommend a national tobacco policy. The panel would conduct a series of open hearings on Capitol Hill, just as if it were an actual congressional committee.

Our shadow committee had precisely the intended effect. The Clinton White House and the news media recognized the enormous credibility that Kessler and Koop brought to the subject, and treated the proceedings as being vitally important to the fate of the agreement. In July, the advisory committee declared the proposed agreement "unacceptable" and laid out a much stronger alternative plan to control smoking. The White House immediately began distancing itself from the original settlement. The committee also had a powerful impact in the Senate. As details of the shortcomings became public, John McCain started insisting on changes that strengthened his bill, alarming the tobacco industry, which spent tens of millions of dollars to kill it, and prompting the Republican leadership to abandon it. By September, the settlement was effectively dead.

OVER THE NEXT DECADE, THE TOBACCO WARS DRAGGED ON IN Congress and the courts. The industry reached a $206 billion Master Settlement Agreement in 1998 that ended the state lawsuits. The following year, the Clinton Justice Department sued for additional billions for conspiracy to defraud and mislead the public about the health effects of smoking. But even the full might of the federal government could not rob Big Tobacco of its Washington clout. In 2000, the U.S. Supreme Court ruled 5–4 that the FDA lacked the authority to regulate tobacco as an addictive drug, putting the burden on Congress to pass a law granting such authority. Here, tobacco made its stand. Where once it had barely distinguished between the parties, the industry increasingly allied with Republicans during the 1990s. When George W. Bush took office in 2001, giving the GOP full control of the White House and Congress, political progress on tobacco slowed to a crawl. That the industry could still jam the gears of government despite all we had done to weaken it was an illustration of just how entrenched it remained.

But its legal and public relations woes continued to mount. Powerful interest groups follow a pattern as they decline. Overt political force and intimidation gradually give way to obstruction and denial. When the facts have become clear and the scrutiny overwhelming, when the last wisp of uncertainty has evaporated, then defeat looms and they scramble to salvage what they can.

In 2004, partly as a way of trying to salvage its public image, the nation's largest tobacco company, Philip Morris, reversed its stance on regulation and endorsed a bipartisan bill giving the FDA jurisdiction. (The rest of the industry remained opposed, charging that Philip Morris was simply seeking to lock in its favorable market position.) After marrying the regulation to a $12 billion, ten-year program to buy out tobacco growers hard pressed by a dwindling market, the Senate overwhelmingly approved the bill. Economic necessity, rather than direct political pressure, cinched the deal. But years of negative publicity, much of it generated by Congress, had brought this about by thinning the ranks of smokers. "I think FDA regulation is a bad idea," Senator Jim Bunning, the Kentucky Republican, said. "But my growers are in dire straits and they need help."

House Republicans remained hostile to the idea and refused to take action on a counterpart to the Senate bill. Their relationship with tobacco was so tight that when Tom DeLay, their majority leader, was indicted on conspiracy charges by a Texas grand jury in 2005, he flew to his arraignment on a plane owned by R. J. Reynolds Tobacco. But after Republicans lost control of the House in the 2006 election, tobacco's grip weakened. The following year, Tom Davis and I introduced the Family Smoking Prevention and Tobacco Control Act, giving the FDA regulatory authority and ensuring that tobacco is not advertised or sold to children. In July 2008, the bill had such strong support that it easily cleared the House. A veto threat from President Bush and Republicans' determination to filibuster prevented the Senate from taking action. But by now, it was only a matter of time.

ONE OF THE GREATEST TRAVESTIES THAT I HAVE WITNESSED DURing my long career was the government's failure to assert jurisdiction over the most deadly product sold in America. From the moment I arrived in Congress anyone who cared to look could see that our nation's health depended on congressional action to confront the threat from smoking. Year after year cigarettes killed millions of people.

The tobacco industry operated in a realm beyond ordinary corporate responsibility. Our government forbids manufacturers of things like automobiles, food, and drugs from recklessly endangering consumers. When they do so, they're called to account. We don't allow them to suppress evidence, ignore scientific research, or continue following whatever pattern of behavior has caused harm, and we demand that their executives explain themselves before Congress and the public.

Yet for decades, Big Tobacco managed to avoid these basic requirements.

At first, its enormous power foreclosed the very possibility of major legislation. Instead, we attacked tobacco's public image and incrementally improved the law—on warning labels, smokeless tobacco, and airplanes—however and wherever we could. But ultimately it was oversight, rather than legislation, that made the greatest impact on our nation's relationship to tobacco.

Cigarette smoking remains the leading preventable cause of death in the United States; worldwide it kills more than five million people each year. But the percentage of the U.S. population that smokes has fallen steadily, from 37 percent of all adults in 1974 to fewer than 20 percent in 2007. Even more important is the trend among kids. Since the late 1970s, the percentage of high school seniors who smoke daily has fallen by nearly two-thirds. And since 1991, when researchers first started keeping track, the percentage of eighth-graders who smoke has dropped by more than half.

Tobacco continues to kill at an alarming rate. But the prospects for change are brighter than at any time since I've been in Congress. On January 21, 2009, a fellow struggling ex-smoker took the oath of office, shifting the dynamics of the tobacco fight once again, this time likely with historic repercussions. Soon after Barack Obama became our forty-fourth president, and thirty years after I began my push for tougher legislation, the House and Senate began work on a comprehensive bill authorizing the FDA to at last regulate nicotine in cigarettes—a bill that President Obama has promised to sign.

CHAPTER 10

Steroids and
Major League Baseball

DURING THE 1990S, MAJOR LEAGUE BASEBALL EXPERI-enced a sharp and unexplained increase in home runs. Long-standing records seemed to fall every week, and a nation of baseball fans watched captivated as stars like Sammy Sosa and Mark McGwire blasted monster shots of a type never seen before. And it wasn't just the cleanup hitters—all of a sudden, every light-hitting infielder seemed to have discovered a home run stroke and previously untapped power. The change was evident beyond the statistics. Players seemed hulkingly bigger. Something was going on.

Baseball fans all over could see what was happening, and many suspected the culprit. Rumors of steroid use had hung over the game for some time. Debates about who was clean and who wasn't became common talk in baseball circles. I was never a part of them—I'm not much of a sports fan. But as the ranking member of the House Government Reform Commit-tee, the evidence of baseball's steroid outbreak appeared to me in a different format. The public health reports that crossed my desk showed an alarming rise in teenage steroid abuse. According to a 2004 study by the Centers for Disease Control and Prevention, more than 500,000 teenagers had used steroids, nearly triple the number just ten years earlier.

In February 2005, former Major League Baseball player Jose Canseco published a memoir, *Juiced: Wild Times, Rampant 'Roids, Smash Hits, and How Baseball Got Big*, describing widespread abuse of performance-enhancing drugs in major league clubhouses that he claimed to have witnessed, and participated in, during his seventeen-year career. The book caused an immediate uproar because he accused many of the game's biggest stars of having taken steroids.

Canseco's charge alarmed me, because the culture of the professional clubhouse invariably becomes the culture of the high school gym. If professional players are using steroids, then college players feel pressure to use them to get to the big leagues, and high school players feel compelled to follow suit to land a scholarship and make the jump to college ball. And indeed, public health reports showed precisely this happening.

But what troubled me most was Major League Baseball's reaction to the allegations. Commissioner Bud Selig dismissed Canseco's charges as "sheer nonsense," and made clear that baseball would not be investigating them. "The commissioner isn't looking backward; he's looking forward," Selig's chief assistant, Sandy Alderson, said shortly after the news broke. "I'd be surprised if there's any significant follow-up."

Accountability is important. And Major League Baseball, a multibillion-dollar, largely self-regulating industry, did not seem to be taking seriously what appeared to be a scandal of epic proportions. There were reasons beyond Canseco's book to suspect that steroid use in professional baseball was a serious problem. The Justice Department had recently handed down indictments in its own investigation of steroid use in professional sports. President Bush, who co-owned a major league team before he became president, thought the issue important enough to have included it in his 2004 State of the Union address. And as every fan knew, the sudden explosion of home runs suggested that something was amiss with the national pastime.

Though it is not well known, Congress had examined this issue once before. In 1973, the House Committee on Interstate and Foreign Commerce conducted a year-long investigation of drugs in professional sports that discovered that they were being used "in all sports and levels of competition. In some instances, the degree of improper drug use—primarily amphetamincs and anabolic sterolds—can only be described as alarming." The committee's chairman, Harley Staggers of West Virginia, was so concerned that a public hearing on those findings would encourage teenagers to experiment with steroids that instead he met privately with the commissioners of all the major sports, urging Baseball commissioner Bowie Kuhn to institute tough penalties and testing. Afterward, satisfied that Kuhn would do so, Staggers issued a press release in which he stated, "Based on the constructive responses and assurances I have received from these gentlemen, I think self-regulation will be intensified, and will be effective." But thirty years later, self-regulation had plainly failed to stop drug abuse.

I suggested to Tom Davis, the Virginia Republican who chaired the Oversight and Government Reform Committee, that we hold a hearing to find out why Major League Baseball wasn't taking a stronger stand. At the same time, we could use the occasion to examine the public health consequences of growing steroid abuse among teenagers. A serious baseball fan, Davis agreed that we should look into Canseco's claims. Since Major League Baseball was disinclined to act, we decided that the committee would take up the task ourselves.

We also agreed that major league players should be among the witnesses called to testify at any hearing. Rumors of heavy steroid use had been swirling for years, and several players had testified to the grand jury in the Justice Department's investigation of a Bay Area laboratory that had supplied many professional athletes. But no player before Canseco had ever given a public account of what everybody seemed to agree was the league's dirty secret. Canseco was therefore an obvious choice to testify, as was his former teammate, Mark McGwire, who was among the players Canseco accused of taking steroids in *Juiced*, and whom we assumed would be eager to rebut the charge under oath. Another, Rafael Palmeiro, had publicly volunteered to testify, so we issued him an invitation. Sammy Sosa, Curt Schilling, and Frank Thomas rounded out the list of star players. Bud Selig and Donald Fehr, the head of the players union, were invited to appear on a separate panel to provide their perspectives.

Major League Baseball greeted the news of our hearing with shock and outrage: How dare we presume to meddle in its affairs! So virulent was the league's opposition to the mere idea of cooperating with us that it hired a former House general counsel to argue that the committee lacked jurisdiction. We reminded him that the House rules state, "the Committee on Government Reform may at any time conduct investigations of any matter," and that the use of performance-enhancing drugs, illegal under the federal Controlled Substances Act, was plainly a matter that fell under our purview. Even so, the league refused to provide a copy of its steroids policy, forcing us to take extraordinary measures. In all the years I spent investigating the tobacco industry—masters of obstruction and refusal to cooperate—never once did I have to issue a subpoena to obtain information. If the industry sensed it was going to lose a fight, it handed over whatever we were after rather than suffer the ignominy of being slapped with a subpoena. But not baseball. On the issue of steroids, the league proved more recalcitrant than Big Tobacco, and compelled us to subpoena documents and testimony.

The clamor was not confined to the league's front office. Given the nature of the scandal and who it involved, the national media—and particularly the sports media—quickly became consumed with it. And at the outset, most people seemed to agree that we were the bad guys. Even Senator John McCain of Arizona, whose Commerce Committee hearing on steroids in 2004 had been the catalyst for baseball's new drug policy, questioned the need for further investigation. The attacks came from every direction: What business did Congress have looking into baseball? Why would we give credence to the claims of Jose Canseco, an admitted cheat and drug user? What did we think we were going to accomplish? Who did we think we were? The hearing was widely assumed to have no higher motive than the lofty institutional arrogance of media-hungry lawmakers, a notion the league and its lawyers were all too happy to encourage. Many commentators criticized us, even while agreeing that steroids were "a black eye for baseball" that was "ruining the game." Almost no one thought to look at steroids from the perspective of public health.

In February of 2005, the league's stance on performance-enhancing drugs was that, while it might have been a bit slow in recognizing the problem, it had implemented, just weeks before, a tough new policy that it claimed would catch, and severely punish, any offenders. Bud Selig declared, "My job is to protect the integrity of the sport and solve a problem. And I think we've done that." The league emphasized that under the new policy first-time violators would be publicly identified and suspended without pay for ten days. "The fact is," Selig said, "that it is announced and everybody in America will know who it is. That's a huge deterrent." In meetings with us, senior baseball officials described the policy as the "gold standard" and contended, publicly and privately, that given this tough new approach, there was no need for Congress or anyone else to look into the past.

But even before the hearing, it became clear that many of the claims Major League Baseball was making about the strength of its new steroids policy simply weren't true. When the league finally produced the subpoenaed copy of the policy, just three days before we convened on March 17, the language differed markedly from what had been described. Rather than mandating an immediate fine, suspension, and public disclosure, the rules decreed that a positive test for steroids would draw *either* "a 10-day suspension *or* up to a $10,000 fine," a second violation "a 30-day suspension *or* up to a $25,000 fine," a third "a 60-day suspension *or* up to a $50,000 fine," a fourth "a one-year suspension *or* up to a $100,000 fine," and, if a player persisted to a fifth, it would be left entirely to the commissioner's discretion how to deal with him. Given that a number of major league players earn more than $100,000 *per game*, that hardly seemed a daunting penalty.

The list of banned substances did not include many of the steroids prohibited by the International Olympic Committee. Implementation, as well as any decision to ban more drugs, was to be overseen not by independent experts (as with the Olympics) but by a four-member committee of management and labor officials. The policy allowed players an unsupervised hour of grace between their being notified of a test and having to provide a urine sample, which would give violators ample time to take masking agents or other measures to avoid testing positive. Strangest of all, one clause of the policy stated that "all testing . . . shall be suspended immediately" should the government launch an independent investigation. Rather than the strict "one strike and you're out" standard portrayed to the media by baseball officials, the actual policy seemed designed to allow the league to continue covering up or at least minimizing the problem of steroids, while talking tough about its principles. The potential for abuse was obvious.

A truism about lawmaking and oversight is that high-profile issues tend to be much harder to manage than those that don't attract a lot of attention. This can be a significant obstacle. In high-visibility hearings (as the steroid inquiry was sure to be), you can never be entirely certain of what will occur and what the media will take away from the event. One way to mitigate this problem, and ensure that at least some media coverage is appropriately directed, is to release a letter in advance of the hearing framing the relevant facts as you'd like them to be considered. On March 16, the day before the big event, the committee issued a public letter to Selig and Fehr laying out the many discrepancies between the policy they had described and the thing itself.

Rarely is the precise moment at which public opinion shifts so pinpoint-clear as it was in the case of baseball's steroids policy. As soon as the letter went out, members of the media and Congress alike realized they had been misled. They could see for themselves the significant disparity, and many felt personally affronted. No one likes to be duped.

The letter had the intended effect, which was fortunate—because while the next day's hearing seized national attention and forever changed the way the public thinks about steroids and baseball, the focus quickly became the players rather than the policy. While Canseco repeated his claims, and Palmeiro, Sosa, and Schilling denied using steroids, Mark McGwire refused to say whether he had used them or not, repeatedly insisting, "I'm not here to talk about the past." To the national media, and to millions of Americans who watched the hearings on television or listened on the radio, McGwire's equivocation was treated as a clear—and astonishing—admission that he had indeed abused steroids, and opened up the possibility that many other of the game's heroes might have, too. This impression was heightened a few months later when it was revealed that Palmeiro had tested positive for anabolic steroids just weeks after the hearing, slamming the brakes on what had seemed till then a Hall of Fame career.

While the frenzy resulting from the players' testimony was unavoidable, my one regret is that more attention wasn't given to the day's first panel, which examined the devastating effects of teenage steroid use. Among the witnesses were the parents of Taylor Hooten and Rob Garibaldi, aspiring young baseball players who had killed themselves after abusing steroids. Donald Hooten searingly described how his seventeen-year-old son, a star pitcher, turned into another person after his junior varsity coach told him that he needed to "get bigger." Taylor Hooten got bigger all right, gaining thirty pounds of muscle. But he also became angry and depressed, and ultimately hanged himself in 2003. Addressing the major-leaguers seated in the gallery behind him, Donald Hooten said, "Players that are guilty of taking steroids are not only cheaters—you are cowards."

Denise Garibaldi told us how her son had begun using steroids as an eighteen-year-old high school player, won a baseball scholarship to the University of Southern California, and competed in the College World Series. Rob Garibaldi had worshipped Mark McGwire, videotaping the slugger's games on television and breaking down his swing "frame by frame" to emulate it. Steroid use brought him severe psychiatric problems that his father, Raymond, described as "mania, depression, short-term memory loss, uncontrollable rage, delusional and suicidal thinking, and paranoid psychosis." Eventually Rob was kicked off the USC team and lost his scholarship. When confronted, said his father, he responded, "I'm on steroids, what do you think? Who do you think I am? I'm a baseball player, baseball players take steroids. How do you think [Barry] Bonds hits all his home runs? How do you think all these guys do all this stuff? You think they do it from just working out normal?" Rob shot himself in the head in 2002 at the age of twenty-four. "There is no doubt in our mind that steroids killed our son," Denise Garibaldi told the committee.

SOME HEARINGS HAVE A DISPROPORTIONATE IMPACT ON THE NA-tional culture, and this was one of them. The reaction was visceral. Suddenly, just about everyone agreed that this was a problem that had to be addressed. Major League Baseball had been given an opportunity to present and defend its steroids policy—Selig, Fehr, and the league's medical adviser, Dr. El-liot J. Pellman, all testified—and the overwhelming conclusion was that the league had failed miserably. To his credit, John McCain revised his earlier position and concluded that Con-gress might indeed need to intervene in professional baseball. "It just seems to me they can't be trusted," he said after the hearing. "We ought to seriously consider . . . a law that says all professional sports have a minimum level of performance-enhancing drug testing."

Ordinarily, a committee is fortunate to get any live feed of a hearing on C-SPAN. CNN might give parts of a really big one, such as that featuring the tobacco CEOs, live coverage. But the steroid hearing ran gavel-to-gavel not just on cable news sta-tions but on ESPN television and radio. And the unexpected twist of McGwire's testimony ensured that the subject was a mainstay of sports talk radio shows for weeks.

This was significant because the discussion reached an entirely different audience than the one that usually pays at-tention to congressional hearings. Though it did not generate nearly the number of headlines as the players' testimony, the panel with the Hootens and the Garibaldis registered with millions of parents, many of them undoubtedly unaware, as those two stricken families had been, that steroids were a rampant and growing danger to their kids that might warrant a much closer and more thoughtful look. Framing the issue in this way went to the heart of its public health aspect and got people to think about steroids in a different way than they were accustomed to. The problem was not merely "the integrity of the game," but also the health and well-being of American kids.

AFTER THE HEARING, TOM DAVIS AND I DECIDED TO INTRODUCE legislation exactly along the lines that McCain had suggested, while McCain introduced an identical bill in the Senate. The Clean Sports Act of 2005 would authorize the Office of National Drug Control Policy to enact a tough, uniform standard for all professional sports and require commissioners to institute stringent testing policies and penalties for players who test positive. We continued to meet periodically with league representatives to do the two vital things we had been asking them to do all along: to compile a report that took full account of the unwholesome years that were already becoming known as baseball's Steroid Era, and to institute a drug policy with real teeth. But baseball officials still seemed to think that they could tough it out and stave off any serious changes.

It wasn't until November, when it became clear that the House and Senate were going to move forward on the Clean Sports Act, that the league finally ceased its brinkmanship and committed to the kind of meaningful reforms that were needed, announcing several months later that former Senate Majority Leader George Mitchell would conduct an independent investigation into the use of performance-enhancing drugs in the major leagues.

Over the next two years, while Mitchell's investigators were at work, steroids never faded from the public spotlight. The ongoing saga of the Bay Area Laboratory Co-Operative (BALCO), the company at the heart of the Justice Department's investigation of illegal performance-enhancing drugs in professional sports, produced a steady stream of headlines, as the names of star athletes alleged to have used its products leaked out. These included such high-profile ballplayers as Gary Sheffield, Jason Giambi, and, most infamously, Barry Bonds. Then, on November 15, 2007, Bonds was indicted for perjury and obstruction of justice in his grand jury testimony about BALCO. For a moment, it seemed the clamor could get no louder—until, on December 13, George Mitchell submitted his report, and the controversy exploded anew.

Officially the *Report to the Commissioner of Baseball of an Independent Investigation into the Illegal Use of Steroids and Other Performance Enhancing Substances by Players in Major League Baseball*, the Mitchell Report, as it pretty much had to be called, was highly critical of both the league and the players union for having tolerated a culture of drug abuse. The report identified eighty-nine players alleged to have used steroids, among them some of the biggest stars in the game. None was bigger than Roger Clemens, the seven-time Cy Young Award winner. After several days of awkward silence, Clemens issued an emphatic denial through his attorneys that he had ever used drugs.

The Government Reform Committee had scheduled a hearing on January 15, 2008, for Senator Mitchell to present his findings and offer testimony. In the weeks leading up to the hearing, Clemens and his attorneys repeatedly attacked and sought to undermine the Mitchell Report. Here we had such starkly contrasting statements—Mitchell's conclusion that Clemens had used steroids, based on interviews with Clemens's own trainer, Brian McNamee, who admitted having obtained them and specifically to having injected Clemens with them, and Clemens's fervent denial of the charge—that only a hearing in which all parties testified under oath seemed likely to resolve the standoff. Having pushed so hard for an independent report, I thought it was important to find out if the most publicized charge could possibly be inaccurate.

As the committee's investigators obtained depositions in advance of the hearing, a fuller picture began to emerge of just what steroids had been doing to professional baseball. Some players, like Clemens, flat-out denied the allegations and cast aspersions on the report. But many others provided admirable and even moving examples of how to acknowledge and atone for a mistake. Chuck Knoblauch brought his three-year-old son to his deposition, where he corroborated McNamee's charge and admitted to having used human growth hormone (HGH). Knoblauch explained that he wanted to teach his son that when you do something wrong you have to admit to it and face the consequences.

Andy Pettitte, a close friend of Clemens's, who, like Knoblauch, stood accused by McNamee of having used HGH, also confessed to the charge. Pettitte viewed his dereliction in religious terms and expressed the wish to give a full accounting of what he had done. He offered what was clearly a genuine and heartfelt deposition, confessing to several things that our investigators would have had no way of discovering, including the fact that his father had supplied him with HGH. He also told us of a conversation he'd had with Clemens in which Clemens admitted to using HGH. After the deposition, we told Pettitte that we were prepared to redact certain portions of his testimony, so that he could keep his father's role private. But both father and son insisted that the committee release the entire unredacted testimony and lay out the full scope of their actions.

As our investigation proceeded, a seemingly obscure issue gained importance. Clemens told us that he had evidence disproving the Mitchell Report's assertion that he had visited Jose Canseco's Florida home in June 1998, when his team, the Toronto Blue Jays, was in town to play the Florida Marlins. McNamee insisted that Clemens had indeed been there—and that he vividly recalled Canseco's wife comparing breast augmentations with Clemens's wife. If Clemens was right, it would cast serious doubt on McNamee's veracity. So began one of the more unusual inquiries in my career. Committee investigators tracked down the now former Mrs. Canseco, a model and minor celebrity, and Clemens's former nanny, whom McNamee recalled seeing at the party. Both confirmed key elements of McNamee's account.

As the hearing approached, and the hysteria surrounding Clemens reached fever pitch, Tom Davis and I had second thoughts about having Clemens and McNamee testify, sensing that a public appearance might go badly for Clemens and believing that the depositions we had collected—including a four-hour interview with Clemens—provided more than enough material to produce a compelling committee report that supported Mitchell's conclusion. But when we informed Clemens's legal team that we were willing to consider issuing a report in lieu of a hearing, they nevertheless insisted on going forward, emphasizing that Clemens himself felt strongly about having an opportunity to convince the world of his innocence.

In the days leading up to the hearing, Clemens's lawyers pursued the rather unorthodox strategy of attacking me personally and making several provocative comments about the government investigators assigned to the case. Clemens himself embarked on a goodwill tour of Capitol Hill, going office to office shaking members' hands and signing autographs for many of the same lawmakers who would soon be questioning him. The next day's testimony was carried live on practically every cable network, ESPN reprising its wall-to-wall television and radio coverage. For several hours, Clemens and his lawyers lobbed charges at McNamee and sparred with members of the committee. It was never clear to me, then or now, what Clemens imagined he was going to get out of this. But the new evidence presented against him only strengthened the impression that he was obfuscating. In the end, his testimony was widely judged a disastrous self-inflicted wound, and his reputation seems forever marred.

SHORTLY AFTER THE GOVERNMENT REFORM COMMITTEE FIRST ANnounced plans to investigate steroid use in the big leagues, Tom Davis and I responded to the umbrage of the league's attorney in a letter on behalf of the committee explaining our intentions and the reasons for our actions. "We are fans of baseball and admirers of professional baseball players," we wrote. "But Major League Baseball and professional baseball players should not be above responsible scrutiny. We believe that Major League Baseball and baseball players should not be singled out for unfair or punitive treatment. But at the same time, baseball and ballplayers do not, by virtue of their celebrity, deserve special treatment or to be placed above the law."

Baseball is an American institution. But by the time Jose Canseco's book came out it had become clear that the institution's tradition of self-regulation had faltered. This lack of oversight, and the tacit complicity of owners, players, and management, had consequences that reached far beyond the professional sphere. Steroids had become a drug problem that affected not only elite athletes, but also the neighborhood kids who idolize them. In 2004, the Centers for Disease Control and Prevention reported that one out of every sixteen teenagers had used illegal steroids, some of them when they were only in the eighth grade. The willful blindness of Major League Baseball was not the only reason for this. But it was a big part of the reason. The league had a responsibility to do the right thing, a responsibility that it had flagrantly neglected.

Issues like this make it clear why it is important that Congress's powers of oversight extend beyond the government. They also show why Congress does not always need to pass legislation in order to bring about dramatic change. In the wake of the hearings and the Mitchell Report, Major League Baseball and the players union agreed on a much tougher drug policy, adopting many of the recommendations that Mitchell had laid out.

Baseball has by no means eradicated performance-enhancing drugs. Many people suspect that HGH, for example, which does not lend itself to easy testing, continues to pose a problem. But the league seems at last to have moved beyond the Steroid Era. While no one can precisely measure the prevalence of steroid use in baseball, a clear pattern of decline seems evident from recent data. As Peter Gammons of ESPN has noted, the Elias Sports Bureau, which tracks baseball statistics, reported that 2.01 home runs were hit per game in 2008, down almost 10 percent from 2006, and the lowest ratio since 1993. The days when muscle-bound players like Mark McGwire and Barry Bonds would club seventy or more home runs in a season seem to have receded into the past. In 2008, Miguel Cabrera led the American League in home runs by hitting thirty-seven; Ryan Howard led the National League with forty-eight. Overall, professional baseball has gotten younger, smaller, and faster. And as several commentators have noted, baseball players have started looking like baseball players again.

But the most important changes have come in college and high school locker rooms. While we are only beginning to see the studies and statistics, the early evidence is encouraging.

In December 2008, the University of Michigan's Institute for Social Research released its highly regarded annual national survey on teenage drug use. The study, which had tracked a "sharp increase" in male teen steroid use in the late 1990s, now showed the reverse. In 2008, steroid use among twelfth-graders had declined by more than a third over a five-year period; among tenth-graders by more than 40 percent; and among eighth-graders by almost 25 percent. The same study reported that "there has been an increase in the proportion of 12th-grade males . . . who see *great risk* in trying anabolic steroids" (italics in original) and an increase in those who disapprove of peers who do try them.

More so than with almost any other issues in my career—such as tobacco, clean air, or pesticides—I've found that my reasons for looking into steroid use in Major League Baseball have not always been fully understood. While the Government Reform Committee's decision to investigate professional baseball was, and continues to be, primarily looked at as an attempt to clean up professional sports, the broader motivation of protecting kids has gone virtually unnoticed. Thankfully, the effort seems to be succeeding on both fronts. There is much greater awareness today of the dangers steroids pose to teenagers, and education and testing programs instituted by high schools and colleges across the country give me hope that this recent pattern of success will continue.

CONCLUSION

Politics has a strange way of going in cycles. I arrived in Congress a member of the historic "Class of 1974," the first elected after Watergate, and as one of ninety-two mostly Democratic representatives who were swept into office on a message of reform. Americans decided that government under Richard Nixon wasn't working as it should, and they wanted something different.

In 2008, we experienced a similar upheaval, as millions of voters sent Barack Obama to Washington and expanded the Democratic majorities in Congress. The prevailing mood today, as in 1974, is one of great hope for change and reform. The eight years under George W. Bush were an object lesson in why an effective, functional government is necessary. Mired in the worst recession since the 1930s, we now see the cost of systematically dismantling regulation and allowing our government to become the private concern of the well-connected and powerful. Having largely organized our economy around the principle that markets can regulate themselves and still protect the public interest, we have learned again that government must play an active role to ensure that markets work for everyone.

We've arrived at a grim moment, but not one without hope. Throughout my career I have found myself fighting those determined to weaken and undermine government. At times, such as in the early days of the Reagan Revolution, public senti-ment leaned very much against me. But we have now come full circle. Americans see plainly that strong government initiative, just as in the past, is vital to solving the huge problems now weighing on the country and the world.

Growing up in California after the New Deal had changed America so much for the better, my parents instilled in me a sense of how much government can be a force for good. My father liked to remind me that when financial excesses brought on the Great Depression, the federal government stepped in to protect ordinary Americans by regulating Wall Street and imposing a measure of accountability where none had been before, while providing families like ours a path to the middle class by guaranteeing a good education, a secure retirement, and, later on, health care for the poor and elderly. This is a major part of what makes our country great. During my forty years in the California State Assembly and the United States Congress, I have worked to carry on this legacy. Despite its imperfections, our government continues to accomplish great things. I wrote this book to explain how they come about, to share what I've learned, and to illuminate how we made some of the greatest achievements happen.

THE NEW GENERATION OF LEGISLATORS THAT HAS ARRIVED WITH President Obama will learn, as I have, that government is a fine and noble calling, but one that presents constant obstacles and challenges. It is always hard and often thankless to be effective, and it is the nature of our occupation that our successes draw less attention than our failures and the problems we have yet to confront. But good works are always possible.

The struggle for effectiveness is a constant battle. A con-gressman's typical day often seems designed to prevent rather than encourage the processes of making laws and exercising oversight: Major hearings are frequently interrupted by floor votes; different committees on which you sit will hold votes and markups simultaneously; caucus meetings, regional meetings, and constituent demands all vie for your limited time; and many members are pressed by the endless imperative to raise money. It is possible to remain frantically busy from sunrise to sunset without accomplishing anything of significance.

One of the worst pieces of advice routinely given new members of Congress is to "be seen, not heard" and defer to their senior colleagues. Doing precisely the opposite is the surest path to success. Anyone can make a difference right away by finding opportunities to speak out and get involved. Patiently submitting to hierarchy only reinforces the regrettable delusion that nothing of any value can be accomplished by anyone less than a chairman, who can draw on a large staff, the advantage of seniority, and other perquisites of power. I have always admired Al Gore for inviting, while still a junior congressman, a steady stream of experts to his office to talk through the pressing issues of the day. Experts around the world in every field would jump at the chance to brief any member of Congress curious to hear their point of view. Anyone who follows Gore's example can become a respected leader on a given issue long before he picks up a chairman's gavel.

The art of legislating is essentially a process of learning. The key to mastering policy is to first master the facts of an issue, since the best policy always derives from them (and never the other way around). When, for example, the AIDS crisis confronted us in the early 1980s, understanding the basics about the disease was the crucial first step toward a proper legislative response. Only once we understood the scope of the problem could we turn to political considerations and begin looking for opportunities to move a bill. Congress is an imperfect institution, and among its 535 members will always be those who abuse their authority and thwart even the most desperately needed programs. Facts are what ultimately overwhelm them and allow good laws to prevail. The Ryan White CARE Act, though it took nine years to become law, is still doing its quiet good two decades later.

Congress is designed to stop things, not build them. So to block a law is much easier than to pass one. Moving something forward often requires having the subcommittee chairman, committee chairman, and the Democratic and Republican leadership all be in favor of it, which is rarely the case. On almost every issue in Washington there will arise an economic interest set on actively resisting a proposed reform, and this opposition—very likely well funded—will muster lobbyists, public relations firms, and advertising talent to try to stop Congress from acting. The odds are usually stacked against you.

That's one reason why bipartisanship is so important. If the committee process is permitted to work as intended—as it did under chairmen like my early mentor, Paul Rogers—then all points of view will come under consideration as a bill is drafted, which only enhances its prospects. Those who can manage to navigate the arduous legislative process while still preserving the key elements of policy will probably have forged a consensus strong enough to survive the House and Senate, and wise enough to produce a law that will work as intended. I've made a habit of seeking out members of good will with whose views I disagree for exactly this reason: Henry Hyde on abortion, Orrin Hatch on pharmaceuticals, Tom Bliley on pesticides, safe drinking water, and tobacco, and Tom Davis on government procurement. If you can find areas of common interest and figure out how to bridge your differences, the result is usually legislation that truly works. In fact, I can think of no major law that I've had a hand in crafting that hasn't depended upon bipartisan support.

Always look for opportunities. The greatest setback in my career was the Republican takeover of the House after the 1994 election. But losing the majority advantage need not render one useless. Another reason bipartisanship is so useful is that it presents opportunities to accomplish things from the minority. Teaming up with Tom Bliley to persuade Congress to pass the Safe Drinking Water Act in 1995 and pesticide legislation in 1996 created valuable laws. Had the Republican leadership been a little less obstinate, those accomplishments would also include historic tobacco legislation.

Even absent a partner in the majority, simply being in Congress affords one enough power to make an immediate difference. As a minority member of the Government Reform Committee, reading about problems in the newspaper, writing letters to federal agencies asking questions and demanding information, and then releasing the resulting reports to colleagues, constituents, and the media helped move the public debate on issues ranging from drug prices to teacher-student ratios. Any member of Congress can do the same thing.

TO PASS THE KIND OF LANDMARK LAWS THAT FUNDAMENTALLY change society means that you will have to take on, and then overcome, the most powerful special interests. This can lead you into a lonely battle, often against members of your own party whom you otherwise like and admire. But it's essential never to be intimidated or discouraged. One consequence of the conservative campaign against government has been a rise in cynicism and apathy that makes it easier for those interests to operate barely noticed and has convinced many people, including some colleagues of mine, that Congress can't or won't look out for them. Over the years, I've experienced more than enough of these same frustrations myself. But I've also learned that the powers that the Constitution entrusts to every member of Congress are sufficient to protect the public interest. Used wisely, they can even overwhelm seemingly insurmountable foes.

In my own experience, whatever interest I'm up against always seems to have more money, better lawyers, swarms of lobbyists, and the resources to go on fighting for years. But tobacco companies, pharmaceutical makers, utilities, and government contractors share one overriding weakness: They're usually seeking to hide certain central facts in order to maintain some economically advantageous position that makes them money. A sustained effort to air the truth is always the best strategy for defeating them.

One reason major legislation like the Clean Air Act is so difficult to pass is that large industries fight back by issuing what appear to be factual claims of their own, invariably warning of the catastrophe that will befall the industry, or even the entire country, should an unwanted reform be permitted to take effect. For years, utilities and chemical companies maintained that toxic air pollutants were not a problem—until we passed the Toxic Release Inventory and the hard data revealed a huge problem that Congress eventually was able to fix. An even better example is the 1994 bill I introduced banning smoking in restaurants, hotels, and other public places. The tobacco companies joined forces with the restaurant and hospitality associations to warn that if the law were passed, "smoking police" would drive away their clientele and ruin their businesses, leading to widespread bankruptcies and ultimately dragging the country into recession. We countered with data from the Indoor Building Association showing that a smoking ban would in fact save these same establishments millions of dollars a year, because tobacco smoke does tremendous damage to indoor spaces, requiring frequent and costly painting and cleaning, as well as expensive air filters. Several years later, after the ban went into effect, not only had public health improved, but the dire predictions turned out to be nonsense. The crowd still came out, and maintenance costs for hotels, restaurants, and bars plunged dramatically.

As we look ahead to our next set of national challenges, it's vital that we keep these lessons in mind. Opponents of universal health care coverage, climate change legislation, and stronger financial regulation have already begun warning of the calamitous costs that serious reform would impose on an unprepared country. As the legislative process picks up momentum, these calls are sure to intensify.

PATIENCE, A KNACK FOR FINDING ALLIES (ESPECIALLY UNLIKELY ones), and the ability to persevere for very long stretches are the qualities that ultimately distinguish the best legislators. Confronting our biggest problems, like polluted air and pervasive death from smoking, is, if not a lifetime job, very close to a career. It can take years or even decades. But sustained focus and interest, and an ability to seize on openings as they present themselves, will eventually yield success, no matter how dark the present circumstance. The most significant clean air laws in our nation's history took seed in the desperate defense against Reagan's assault on the existing order. For the next decade, our proposals consistently reflected what scientists told us were the greatest threats to the environment: acid rain, toxic air pollutants, ozone depletion. Using oversight hearings to dramatize dreadful lessons like Bhopal and drive home the dangers of inaction, we eventually came away with the Clean Air Act Amendments of 1990. And when, along the way, the science showed accumulating evidence of global warming, we began work on the first climate change bill, which we introduced in 1992. The years of subsequent effort and growing public awareness have laid the groundwork for what could soon become another historic piece of legislation.

The greatest lesson that my time in Congress has taught me is that even though significant achievements often seem likely to be long, hard, and wearying, they are nevertheless possible to bring about. Congress, as it always has, continues to produce important public benefits. Each preceding chapter is the story of a bill or a series of hearings that not only beat the odds by becoming law (or, with steroids, eliminating the need for one), but that, once implemented, has achieved what we set out to do. In some cases, like nutrition labeling or banning smoking on airplanes, the benefits of these laws have become so thoroughly ingrained that they're simply taken for granted or, indeed, the original problem is forgotten altogether. How many people today recall reeking like an ashtray as they disembarked from a long flight? It's amazing how often the most hotly contested issues are instantly forgotten once a good law has taken effect.

In forty years as a legislator, I've seen just about everything. I've worked with people who do a terrible job, watched plenty of good legislation die, and experienced the grinding frustration of being stuck in the minority party for more than a decade. If anybody should be cynical about our government and how it works, I should. But I'm not. Because despite the setbacks and frustrations, what Congress has achieved during my time has made clear to me that if you organize the right people, follow the facts, and force the issue, it is possible, and even likely, that good work can make a difference in the lives of millions of Americans—which, in the end, is a lawmaker's highest purpose.

ACKNOWLEDGMENTS

I want to thank Joshua Green for collaborating with me on this book. We spent many hours together, and he spent many more stitching my stories together. Josh is a superb and talented writer, and I am amazed at how he was able to articulate my thoughts in such a captivating way. I am grateful for the confidence placed in me by my publisher, Jonathan Karp, who thought a book about my experiences might give a different perspective on how Congress does and can work.

I have always felt that the key to success in legislation is having the best staff possible. It has been my great fortune over the years to be assisted by a dedicated and talented group of people who share my commitment and can help push the envelope to achieve results.

I want to single out three people for their instrumental roles in directing the staff and advising me on the legislation I have worked on in my career. I will always be indebted to them for their decades-long friendship and exceptional work: Phil Schiliro, my longtime chief of staff; Karen Nelson, the former staff director for the House Health and Environment Subcommittee who is with me still as the top health aide for the House Energy and Commerce Committee; and Phil Barnett, the former staff director for the House Oversight and Government Reform Committee and current staff director for the House Energy and Commerce Committee.

It has been a rare pleasure to have worked with so many

capable people over the years, and I want to acknowledge the enormous contributions of Bill Corr, Bill Schultz, Rip Forbes, Andy Schneider, Tim Westmoreland, Greg Wetstone, Ruth Katz, Kristin Amerling, David Rapallo, Brian Cohen, Michelle Ash, Greg Dotson, Karen Lightfoot, Pat Delgado, Norah Mail, Becky Claster, Zahava Goldman, Rachel Sher, and Lisa Pinto.

I wrote this book for interested readers, but even more for my family, and I dedicate this book to them. Above all, I dedicate it to my wife and life-partner, Janet, whose love and devotion has been the single best thing that has happened to me; to my daughter, Shai Abramson; to my son, Michael Waxman, and daughter-in-law, Marjorie Waxman; and to my grandchildren, Ari, Maya, and No'a Abramson, and Eva and Jacob Waxman, who mean the world to me.

Joshua Green would like to thank the invaluable Timothy Dickinson, along with Chloe and Alicia, for their love and support.

INDEX

ABOUT TWELVE

TWELVE was established in August 2005 with the objective of publishing no more than one book per month. We strive to publish the singular book by authors who have a unique perspective and compelling authority. Works that explain our culture; that illuminate, inspire, provoke, and entertain. We seek to establish communities of conversation surrounding our books. Talented authors deserve attention not only from publishers, but from readers as well. To sell the book is only the beginning of our mission. To build avid audiences of readers who are enriched by these works—that is our ultimate purpose.

For more information about forthcoming TWELVE books, please go to www.twelvebooks.com.